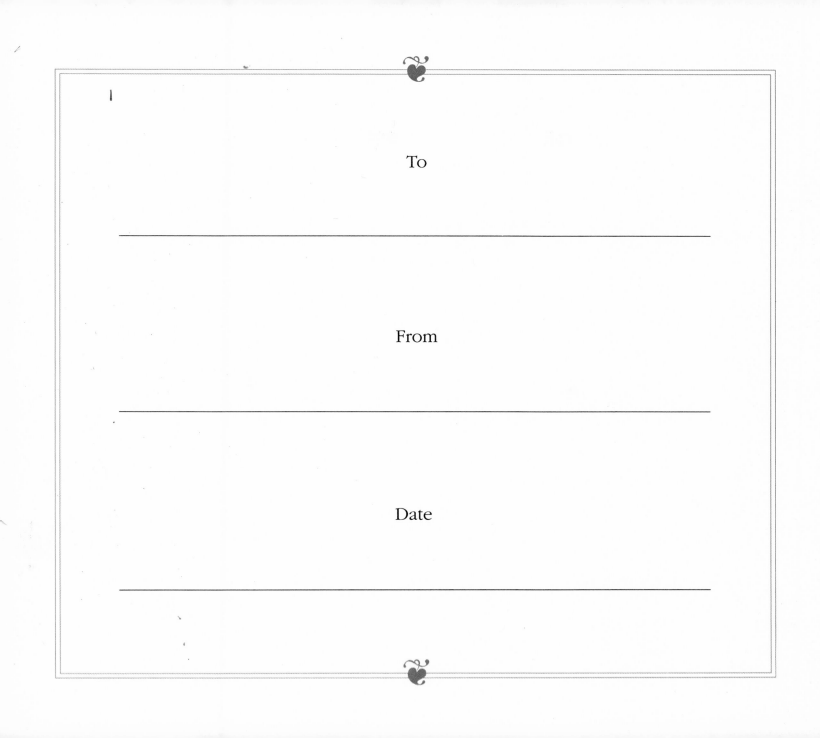

To

_____

From

_____

Date

_____

To Peter, Viveca, and Trevor.
May your hearts be dedicated to God, and may your lives be devoted to the values
described on the following pages.

Train Up A Child

GIVING THE VALUES THAT LAST A LIFETIME

ROLF ZETTERSTEN

WORD PUBLISHING

Dallas·London·Vancouver·Melbourne

TRAIN UP A CHILD

Scripture quotations are from The Holy Bible, New International
Version. Copyright © 1973, 1978, 1984 International Bible Society. Used
by permission of Zondervan Bible Publishers.

The author gratefully acknowledges Alain Boublil Music Ltd. for permission to quote
lyrics in part from RED AND BLACK (THE ABC CAFE) from the musical
"Les Miserables" by Alain Boublil and Claude-Michel Schönberg.
Music by Claude-Michel Schönberg. Lyrics by Alain Boublil, Jean-Marc
Natel, and Herbert Kretzmer. © Alain Boublil Music Ltd. (ASCAP).

Library of Congress Cataloging-in-Publication Data:

Zettersten, Rolf, 1955–
    Train up a child : giving the values that last a lifetime / Rolf
Zettersten.
      p. 2 cm.
    ISBN 0-8499-0874-4 (hard)—ISBN 0-8499-0912-0 (padded)
    1. Child rearing—Religious aspects—Christianity.   2. Moral
development. I. Title
HQ769.3.Z47   1991
248.8'45—dc20   91-24252
                                                CIP

1 2 3 4 9   9 8 7 6 5 4 3 2 1

Printed in the United States of America

Contents

Foreword

These are difficult days for families. Healthy, happy homes seem like sweet memories of some faraway place and time. Parents who manage to remain married struggle with weighty burdens of finance, schedule, morality, and spirituality. Frequently, they have little time for their children, so demanding is their lifestyle. Even in "better" neighborhoods, latch-key kids wander after school, lonely and bored. Tragically, more than half the time, divorce shatters homes, and single parents desperately try to serve as both mother and father, provider and comforter, teacher and spiritual mentor.

To make matters worse, groups who identify themselves as "child advocates" propose changes in our society that can only damage and destroy the generations to come. Moral and spiritual values of minor children are being eroded, and some of the basic responsibilities of caring parents are being viewed as restrictive, and even abusive.

Is there any hope for our children and grandchildren? Of course there is!

"Train up a child in the way he should go, and when he is old he will not depart from it"—so says the ancient Hebrew proverb. Even in the best of circumstances, training up children has never been simple. It wasn't easy in the days of King Solomon, who penned that hopeful proverb thousands of years ago. And it isn't easy now.

I can't think of anyone who is more aware of the challenges and requirements of successful parenting in the 1990s than Rolf Zettersten. His vantage point as executive vice-president at

Dr. James Dobson's ministry, Focus on the Family, has given him a unique perspective on Christian family life in today's world. I admire and respect Rolf, not just because he's a close friend and occasional fishing buddy, but because I believe he is extremely aware of today's trends in parenting across the nation and around the world. He is able to analyze and describe what we are doing for our children, and he can help us to be better parents at the same time. *Train Up a Child* allows Rolf to serve skillfully both as observer and well-seasoned adviser, offering up a wonderful collection of images, impressions, and invaluble insights.

Parents who follow the Christian path have the heartwarming privilege of presenting priceless spiritual gifts to their children. As you read, you will discover nine of these treasures—each one a distinctive token of parental love. You will be given biblical background for these nine principles, learning why they are so very important to God. And you will delight in true-life illustrations drawn from a montage of family portraits, both past and present. Words of wisdom are drawn from such beloved instructors as Dr. James Dobson, Chuck Swindoll, Charles Stanley, and Jamie Buckingham. Within these pages is an expression of Christian family life that promises each reader new inspiration and encouragement.

What do we have to offer our boys and girls? A great deal indeed, says Rolf. Love. Truthfulness. Industriousness. Commitment. And much, much more. The well-worn adage contends that "the family that prays together, stays together." We must pray—and more. The values our Heavenly Father has always entrusted to His people are the greatest heritage we can impart to our offspring. And these values, like stones dropped into deep waters, will send their ripples outward, blessing child after child, family after family, generation after generation.

Gary Smalley
President
Today's Family

Introduction

A few years ago, Dr. Tim LaHaye published an interesting chart in his Family Life Seminars book, *You and Your Family*. The chart diagrammed the legacy of two men who lived in the eighteenth century. The first was Max Jukes, an alleged profligate and moonshiner. He never went to church and married a woman of like mind. The second was Dr. Jonathan Edwards, a godly minister who was credited with igniting the Great Awakening through his sermons. He also married a woman who shared his philosophies and faith.

Of Max Jukes' 1,026 descendants: 300 died prematurely, 100 were sent to prison, 190 were prostitutes, and 100 were known drunks. Of Dr. Edwards' 729 descendants: 300 were preachers, 65 were college professors, 13 were authors, 3 were congressmen, and 1 was vice-president of the United States.

Scripture teaches us about generational continuity, a concept that our actions and prayers will yield a harvest in the lives of our children, grandchildren, and the generations to come. I know this is true. I have seen it validated through the experiences of others, and I have watched it work in my own family as well.

On a shelf in my office rests an unassuming little book that holds great significance for me. It was published in 1958 in Swedish. Between its plain blue covers are 120 meaningful pages written by my grandfather, Birger Zettersten. Entitled *All by Grace*, it conveys the ideas, thoughts, and deeds of this man who devoted his existence to preaching the Gospel. I am reminded by this book just how much his life has shaped the lives of his descendants. He died in 1957 when I was two years old. Although I never met him, his influence affects me now—more than thirty-five years later and half a world away.

To one extent or another, we all live out the heritages of those who have gone before us. The habits, decisions, and values of our ancestors have tremendous implications for our lives. Of course, that implies something very significant when we become parents today, because it suggests that we are responsible for future generations as well as our own children.

I don't know about you, but that thought wears me out! Please, Lord, let me raise one generation at a time. Parenting my kids is hard enough without having to worry about the descendants they create with future in-laws.

I really don't believe that God requires us to assume that burden. He only asks us to obey him and teach his commandments to our offspring. And blessings will flow from that fountain for years to come.

How can we start that process? We begin by demonstrating our faith as an example to our own children. Along the way, we look for opportunities to teach them concrete absolutes which will give structure to what they have observed in our lifestyle.

What values do we select? To help identify those principles, I solicited the help of other parents. Through the platform of *Focus on the Family* magazine, I asked mothers and fathers to share the most important precepts they want their children to learn. As a result of this process, I defined a list of nine enduring values. You'll find them described and explored in the following chapters.

Admittedly, this was not a scientific survey administered according to standardized research methodology. And I wouldn't argue that this list is even complete; certainly other characteristics could be added.

But these values, which form the outline for this book, have something else going for them. They represent the collective wisdom of hundreds of parents. These principles are timeworn, tested, proven, and forged on the anvil of experience. Best of all, they are based in scripture.

At the outset of this book, allow me to gratefully acknowledge the contributions of these parents whose input shaped the contents. They are my collaborators. Let me also thank Jan Johnson, my editor, as well as my friends at Word Publishing.

I hope and pray that in the following pages you will find inspiration and guidance to instill some significant values in the lives of your children. And by so doing, you will begin or continue a legacy of spiritual qualities that will be passed on to future generations within your family.

Thest commandments that I give
you today are to be upon your hearts.
Impress them on your children.
Talk about them when you sit
at home and when you walk
along the road, when you lie
down and when you get up.

Deuteronomy 6:6-7

Teach Your Children Well

Being a parent is the most incredible and important job on earth. When we accept this role, we embark on a journey that will lead us to the highest thrills, the deepest burdens, and the greatest rewards this human experience can offer. Parenthood also brings us daunting challenges that will push us to the limits of our skills and abilities. When I consider the tremendous, yet significant task of parenthood, I am reminded of a newspaper account from a few years back of a pilot in Titusville, Florida, who had spent years constructing, fine-tuning, and polishing an antique prop plane. One afternoon, he decided to take his cherished, vintage biplane for a flight.

After carefully positioning his plane on the runway, he went to the nose of the aircraft and spun the propeller. The engine sputtered for a few seconds and then settled into a sweet idle as all of the cylinders began firing. The pilot kicked the blocks from under the tires and was making his way around the plane when something unexpected happened.

Suddenly, the aircraft bolted forward and proceeded down the runway. It quickly gained speed and in a few moments was airborne. The hapless pilot stood forlorn on the tarmac and watched his plane circle overhead before it headed out toward the Atlantic Ocean. He never saw his beloved plane again!

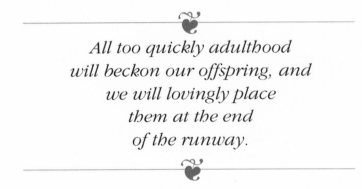

All too quickly adulthood will beckon our offspring, and we will lovingly place them at the end of the runway.

This amusing, yet tragic, story is much like raising a child. As moms and dads, we pour our energies and emotions into the growth and development of our offspring. This effort, which can span two decades or more, requires constant vigilance and untiring labor.

Our objective is to provide for our kids' well-being, but parents define success in different ways. For example, some moms and dads place the highest priority on physical health and financial freedom. One popular quarterback currently playing in the National Football League illustrates this point. Although he has succeeded through hard work and the development of his own abilities, he is largely the product of his father's master plan. When the little guy was born, his dad decided that he would eventually become a star athlete.

The toddler was raised on a strict diet that prohibited sugar and other fattening foods. He had an exercise regimen and a physical training program throughout his childhood. He was introduced to sports at an early age, and his dad worked with him for years to develop his skills. Today, that goal has been achieved and dad's dreams are fulfilled.

Other parents emphasize mental and social development. Remember the movie *Baby Boom?* Mothers and fathers were desperate to enroll their kids in New York's most prestigious preschools to give them a head start in life. In one memorable scene, a dejected mom broke down in tears when she admitted to her snobby friends that her baby was not accepted for admission to a trendy preschool. What a shame! Her child was labeled as a failure at the age of two.

We all want our children to become healthy adults from the physical, mental, and emotional standpoints. But Christian parents want more! None of the other goals matter if our children aren't healthy from a *spiritual* perspective.

Toward this end, we take every precaution to prepare our children for the inevitable day when they will leave our nest. Countless hours of bedtime prayers, inestimable numbers of Bible stories, many years of Sunday school attendance, continuous summers spent at summer camp, Vacation Bible School, and regular outings with the church youth group - all of these efforts reflect our desire to "train up a child in the way he should go."

All too quickly, adulthood will beckon our offspring, and we will lovingly place them at the end of the runway. We'll help them start their engines and kick the blocks out from under their tires. And then, as much as we want to jump in the pilot's seat, we must stand back and watch. At that moment we will know if eighteen years of training and building have paid off. Sure, their little planes may circle and wobble a bit. But hopefully, they will have a successful flight through life.

I thought about a parent's role as trainer when my wife, Linda, gave birth to our third child. Our little Trevor Daniel arrived three weeks prematurely and had several complications as a result. His first few days outside the womb were rough ones. The nurses had drawn blood from his tiny arm and pricked his heel so often that those areas had turned black and blue. He was blindfolded to protect his eyes from the ultraviolet rays in the incubator, and an IV was inserted in his foot.

One afternoon, as I stood next to him, I asked God to touch him physically. "Heal him and let us bring him home," I prayed. I trusted that the Lord would answer my petition. And then I repeated a prayer that I had uttered many times while Trevor was still in the womb:

Let him grow to become a man of God, and give us the wisdom to show him the way. May he have a hunger for you, Lord, and your Word. Help him to experience the fulfillment of knowledge and the rewards of hard work. Let his days be filled with laughter and play, and give him the protection of good Christian companions. Instill in him the ingredients for healthy self-esteem so he has the confidence to reach for his dreams and to reach out to others in need. We dedicate this little one to you and ask you to give him all the richness of a life in Christ.

A few days later, our physician told us that we could take Trevor home. My first prayer was answered, and he has been a healthy baby ever since. We are working with the Lord now to fulfill the second prayer. We won't know the outcome of this request so quickly, but we are prepared to pour our lives and our values into this little one to train him for the next eighteen years. And with God's help, he will succeed.

Protecting Our Children

One night while dining with friends, I saw something I shall never forget. We had just finished our meal and were engaged in a lively conversation when we were interrupted by a commotion at the next table.

We turned and saw a small boy, who looked to be about seven years old, choking on a piece of food. The poor youngster was absolutely incapable of helping himself. His eyes were wide with terror. He uttered no sound as he waved his hands excitedly. Seconds seemed like minutes. His frantic parents desperately tried every maneuver and technique they knew. They pressed on his stomach, patted his back, and poked their fingers down his throat.

Perhaps it was a combination of these efforts, or maybe it was an answer to someone's prayer. Suddenly, the food was dislodged and the boy was saved. He coughed and, with his first breath, let out a high-pitched scream that filled the restaurant. Tears streamed down his little cheeks, and he yelled these telling words which must have been bottled up inside of him throughout the ordeal: "Please, Mama, don't let me die!"

His mother comforted him as he cried, and she gently assured him that he was out of danger. As I reflected on this drama and the frightened boy's first words, I was reminded of how totally dependent our children are upon us as parents.

From a child's point of view, life is full of perils and mysteries. Who has the answers to these dilemmas? Mom and Dad, of course. Our offspring look to us for protection and direction through life's experiences. This simple truth applies to the spiritual as well as the physical aspects of our existence.

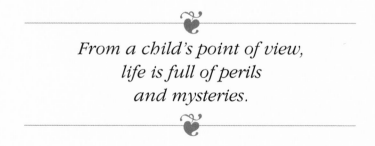

*From a child's point of view,
life is full of perils
and mysteries.*

There is much evidence to suggest that parents, whether they are religious or not, recognize their responsibility to provide some type of spiritual training for their children. A recent article in the December 17, 1990 issue of *Newsweek*, entitled "A Time to Seek," described a phenomenal surge in church attendance. What has caused this sudden growth?

Apparently a large number of baby boomers, people born between 1946 and 1965, are returning to church in order to give their children a bedrock of values. The article said, "Above all, the return to religion is fueled by the boomers' experiences of becoming parents—and the realization that children need a place where they can learn solid values and make friends with peers who share them."

According to this research, about 57 percent of the baby boomers—an estimated 43 million people—now attend church. Sanctuaries are swelling with young families who have recognized the need for formal spiritual training.

In a recent speech, Dr. Louis Sullivan, Secretary of Health and Human Services, echoed this concern when he called for a new "culture of character" based on the values, traditions, and institutions that were originally the centerpiece of our society.

Perhaps this return to the church is intuitive to parents who know that their value

system will eventually reap a harvest in the lives of their offspring. I recall an incident in the Civil War that illustrates this point.

At one point in this terrible conflagration, an average of two thousand Union soldiers were dying every week. The bodies of these unfortunate victims were shipped north by train for proper burial. There were so many bodies that a new cemetery was needed to serve as a final resting place for these soldiers.

The responsibility for this cemetery site selection was given to General Montgomery Meigs, whose own son had died in battle in the Shenandoah Valley. So great was his bitterness over this loss that General Meigs chose the Virginia home of a Confederate officer. When the

---

Needed: A new "culture of character" based on the values, traditions, and institutions that were originally the centerpiece of our society.

---

war was over, that officer, General Robert E. Lee, returned to his estate on the banks of the Potomac and saw that it had become Arlington National Cemetery, the Union Army's most hallowed ground.

How ironic that so many of the young men killed by Lee's forces were buried in his front yard. A similar irony exists in the role of parenting. Our deeds, our priorities, our values *will* come home to rest in our front yards through the lives of our children.

Beating within the heart of every decent parent is a desire to set our children on the right course. Even the rock 'n' roll group Crosby, Stills and Nash sang a popular ballad, "Teach Your Children Well." But what values and principles do you teach them? I think many parents, particularly those who have no religious mooring, are at a loss to define these.

Many years ago I attended an inner-city church that had an active outreach program to children in the community. Every Saturday I joined a group of people who went door-to-door throughout the battered neighborhoods of downtown Los Angeles. Our message to those who answered our knock was quite simple: "We would like to take your children to church and teach them about the Bible. Our buses will pick them up and return them home after the service."

The kids were always eager to accept our

offer—even if they weren't familiar with the concept of Sunday school. I remember one

---

Our deeds, our priorities, our values will come home to rest in our front yards through the lives of our children.

---

confused, yet enthusiastic boy who asked me if he could bring his own spray paint and markers. Then I realized that he had misunderstood the offer.

"No," I explained. "I invited you to *ride* on our bus, not *write* on it."

He came anyway, and so did several busloads of other excited children. The enthusiastic response from these youngsters didn't surprise me, but I was always amazed at how perfectly willing the parents were to let us take their kids. Non-Christians, who wouldn't darken the door of a church, didn't hesitate to say, "Yes, my kids will be ready."

These parents often expressed their desire to provide basic spiritual training for their children. Since they didn't adhere to a defined value system themselves, they were at a loss to instruct their kids in this regard. Even practicing Christians struggle with this parental duty.

Certainly we want our children to learn the Ten Commandments and the concepts of Creation and Redemption. But beyond that, what are the most significant values we can impart to our young that will enable them to lead happy and productive lives?

To answer that question I turned to the readers of *Focus on the Family* magazine. We asked them to define the values they cherished most. Hundreds of letters flooded our office from parents who shared stories of their own upbringing and how they are shaping the lives of their children. After spending hours reading through each letter, we developed the following list of nine values, in order of the frequency with which they were mentioned:

1. Love and obey God.
2. Love others.
3. Be honest.
4. Work hard.
5. Be committed to your family.
6. Respect your elders.
7. Attend church.
8. Avoid materialism.
9. Pray and worship.

There is great wisdom behind this simple list, and it will serve as a blueprint for those who desire to teach their children well. I was

---

Passing values from one generation to another is a prescription for a spiritual life.

---

overwhelmed, not only at the response to my call for sharing, but also that so many have such a strong and sure sense of the cumulative good effects of passing values from generation to generation.

One woman wrote that her parents "had the moral and spiritual values that scripture describes in 1 Corinthians 13:4–8 and in Philippians 4:8. I'm sure these principles were transferred from their parents and grandparents—a perfect example of how our lives will affect generations to come."

Another mother described her parents' influence: "They are Christ to me, molding and shaping me into the woman I am today. They are still teaching me how to live and that is the pattern of life I want to share with my children. No one could ask for more, nor should my children expect less from me."

A father concluded his letter by saying, "And, of course I don't plan to keep them to myself. . . . If I can pass them along to my three children, undiminished and untarnished as they were imparted to me, I'll be happy." What a better aspiration and role model for today's men and fathers than the usual aspirations of the world—to succeed in a career and fulfill one's self!

Another dad, a physician, outlined his values on a prescription pad, a concrete reminder that passing values from one generation to another is a prescription for a spiritual life. He wrote about the responsibility to carry one's share in a relationship, to grow to one's highest potential, to be unselfish and generous. Under his signature appeared the words, "Dispense as Written."

I recently heard the story of a father who came upon his son assembling a jigsaw puzzle. What should have taken no more than a few minutes had become a marathon affair. As the poor lad struggled unsuccessfully to match the odd shapes, the father watched with increasing dismay and frustration. "What is wrong with my boy?" he wondered. "Why can't he put two pieces together?"

Suddenly, it dawned on the father that in his son's eagerness to begin the puzzle he had dumped the pieces on the floor and then cast the box aside. By ignoring the box and its picture of the finished puzzle, the boy had thrown away the blueprint for the project!

The father retrieved the box and showed his son the picture of the completed puzzle. After that it didn't take long before the task was successfully completed.

In a sense, that's how I view the list of values described by our survey respondents. They can serve as a blueprint for a meaningful Christian life. If we are interested in actively shaping our kids' lives, then this list, which represents the collective wisdom of many other parents, is a great place to start.

Love the Lord your God
with all your heart and
with all your soul
and with all your mind.

Matthew 22:37

Let My God Be Their God

How do our children view God? Do they see a jovial Sugar Daddy who lavishes gifts and blessings on kids everywhere? Is he a hard-nosed judge who punishes them when they make mistakes? Is he a demanding drill instructor who makes them toe the line of good behavior? Or do they perceive him to be a loving parent who guides them and encourages them to do their best?

A few years ago I read an eight-year-old boy's perspective of God that I found entertaining—and compelling. He wrote:

One of God's main jobs is making people. He makes these to put in the place of the ones that die so there will be enough people to take care of things here on earth. He doesn't make grown-ups. Just babies. I think because they are smaller and easier to make. That way he doesn't have to take up his valuable time teaching them to talk and walk. He can just leave that up to the mothers and fathers. I think it works out pretty good.

God's second most important job is listening to prayers. An awful lot of this goes on, as some people, like preachers and things, pray other times besides bedtime; and Grandpa and Grandma pray every time they eat (except snacks). God doesn't have time to listen to the radio or TV on account of this. As he hears everything, not only prayers, there must be a terrible lot of noise going on in his ears unless he has thought of a way to turn it off. I think we should all be a little quieter.

God sees everything and hears everything and is everywhere—which keeps him pretty busy. So you shouldn't go wasting his time asking for things that aren't important or go over your parents' head and ask for something they said you couldn't have.

While this is somewhat humorous, I actually find this child's understanding of God to be profoundly accurate. Yes, God is certainly very busy. And the youngster has captured several other key truths: God has made us in his image. He listens to us. He is omnipresent and omniscient. He is the ultimate authority—even greater than Mom and Dad!

Apparently, this boy's parents have done a good job of teaching him about our Creator. They obviously realize that a comprehensive understanding of God will lead to a good relationship with him.

This appears to be the objective of many other Christian parents as well. In the informal survey behind this book, I found that knowing and loving God are the most important values parents want to impart to their offspring. This should come as no surprise since Jesus pro-

claimed this to be the First Commandment.

One woman explained her reason for emphasizing this precept of the faith: "The primary value that I want to pass along to my children is a love of God and his word. I want my kids to develop a dependence on our Lord that will strengthen them throughout their lives. As I grow in God's love, I realize how much my relationship with God parallels my relationship with my children. So many qualities I must show my children—patience, mercy, justice— are first demonstrated to me by my heavenly Father. If I am attentive to what God is doing in my life and follow his lead, it will enable me to be what he wants me to be to my children."

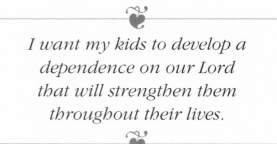

I want my kids to develop a dependence on our Lord that will strengthen them throughout their lives.

This concerned mother echoes the evidence uncovered by recent polls that have explored the priorities of American society. For example, Princeton Survey Research Associates discovered in 1991 that faith in God is by far the most significant part of Americans' lives. They found that 40 percent of those surveyed said they valued their relationship with God above all else, while only 2 percent said a job that pays well was the most important thing in their life.

So it should come as no surprise that parents want to wrap their concept of God in a brightly colored package and place it on the bottom shelf where their kids will reach out and grab it. But that has become an increasingly difficult assignment in today's world. In their book *Children at Risk,* Dr. James Dobson and Gary Bauer have warned that our kids are growing up in a society controlled by people who are indifferent or hostile to the Christian value system. All of the centers of power in our culture (government, public education, the courts, the news media, and the entertainment industry) are now in the hands of a godless minority who use these forums to influence our young.

The effect of this prevailing anti-Christian sentiment has already begun to take its toll on the next generation, which is profoundly ignorant of basic scriptural events or principles. A Gallup Youth Survey asked teenagers three questions about the Bible: (1) Can you name the four gospels of the New Testament? (2) How many disciples did Jesus have? (3) What religious event or happening is celebrated on Easter?

Parents want to wrap their concept of God in a brightly colored package and place it on the bottom shelf where their kids will reach out and grab it.

Sadly, only 20 percent could answer one of those questions. Furthermore, the study revealed that only 15 percent could name one of the Ten Commandments, and only 3 percent could name all ten. I agree with one parent who responded to the survey by saying, "The Bible is like the sheet of directions that comes with a sewing pattern." God gave us the Scriptures to serve as an instruction manual for understanding him. The tragedy is that many kids are being raised without the benefit of Scripture. Thus, if our kids don't know about God's word, then they can never really relate to him. As Christian parents, we want our children to have an intimate relationship with their heavenly Father. Nothing else in life matters if this value is not transferred to the next generation.

One letter from the mother of a disabled child showed how deeply this burden is felt. Writing about her severely physically and mentally limited son, she said, "My child probably will never leave the nest. He will never have any children to pass values on to. So why do I teach him values? God has given a child to us who has severe handicaps. His potential in this life may be extremely limited, but I must be faithful in the task that God has given me to do. There may be no hope for a future with him being independent, but there is that future hope of meeting God face to face."

The Bible is like the sheet of directions that comes with a sewing pattern.

This woman's letter is a lesson that our earthly priorities—growing up, having a family, getting a good job—aren't necessarily the most important ones. I was reminded of this in an-

other way a while back when I attended an NFL game between the Seattle Seahawks and the Los Angeles Raiders. After the game, I visited with some of the players who are special friends to Focus on the Family.

We met just outside the locker room in an area that was not open to the public. Nevertheless, in a few minutes a crowd of people had gathered around one of the popular wide receivers who was completing his final year of a record-breaking career, and several fans were desperately trying to get his autograph. As I watched, I noticed another player who was being edged out of the area by the throng. This player had been the most respected safety in the league just one year before. However, in the last season, he had been platooned for younger talent. Now, as the adoring fans pressed in to see the retiring wide receiver, they pushed right past last year's star. It was a sobering lesson on the fleeting nature of fame. Like ice on a hot stove, today's temporal priorities will melt into obscurity and irrelevance. Only those things of eternal consequence have true value.

This is particularly significant when we face obstacles and barriers. We can learn and teach our children to move toward a relationship with God in times of earthly adversity and setbacks. We can help our children, in their adversity, to know the love of a caring God.

One woman described how she overcame incredible pain through her dependency on the Lord. Many years ago her ten-year-old brother was killed in a senseless act of violence by a drunk driver. She described how her parents' response in that crisis gave her a legacy that will last a lifetime. She still remembers her brother's funeral service where they acknowledged God's love by singing "The Lord's Prayer" and "What a Friend We Have in Jesus." No wonder one of her most important values—for herself and her own grown children—is to remain close to the Lord in every situation.

I recall one occasion when Dr. Dobson expressed so clearly his perspective on what's truly important. We were driving home from a mountain-climbing trip in the Sierra Nevadas where we had enjoyed the fellowship of several other fathers and their children. Spending three days away from the routine of city life had given us an opportunity to reflect on the priorities of our lives. The five-hour drive home gave us ample time to share our feelings about many of the principles important to us. Then we talked about the brevity of life, and Dr. Dobson made this comment: "You know, Rolf, I would feel satisfied if I could achieve just three goals with my life."

"What are they?" I asked.

"First, I want to stand before my Creator and hear the words: 'Well done, good and faithful servant. Enter into the joy of the Lord.'

"Second, I want to take as many people as possible to heaven with me.

"Third, I want to be reunited with my family in heaven. I want to see my parents again. I want Shirley to be there, and I want to spend eternity with my children."

Those goals burn within the hearts of every Christian mom and dad. As we seek to teach our children about God, may we also find ways to show them how they can have a meaningful relationship with him.

ay the Lord make your love increase and overflow for each other and for everyone else, just as ours does for you.

1 Thessalonians 3:12

THREE

The Gift Of Love

One of the marvelous blessings of the Christian life is that we experience God's love most when we share it with others. By expressing our charity through hospitality and compassion, we develop a greater appreciation and realization of the love that caused God to give us his only Son. And when we follow this second greatest commandment ("Love your neighbor as yourself"), we teach our children to become lovers of humankind.

Acts of love can make a particularly profound impression on children. Over and over again people describe fond memories of how their parents opened their homes and hearts to friends and total strangers.

One woman wrote in response to our survey, "I have a deep admiration for my mother when I recall the many occasions when company would appear right at lunchtime or suppertime and she would make them feel that they had received an invitation two weeks before. She would somehow stretch a meal for four into a meal for ten. And she passed on to me the importance of giving and placing others before myself."

This was not a mother who shared her love grudgingly. It is one thing to stretch a meal to accommodate unexpected guests. It is yet another to do it with so much love and hospitality that the latecomers feel as if they had been invited, welcomed, and at home. Is this not what Jesus did when he sat down to eat with the poor, the prostitutes, and the dregs of society?

---

*A nation's values can
be inferred from the aspirations
of its children.*

Many, too, remembered their fathers' acts of kindness. "My father especially loved people," one woman wrote. "He never had an enemy and didn't know a stranger. I had a friend who came from an unfortunate home situation. I would invite her to spend the night with us quite often. My dad would make her feel like she belonged in our family."

This man went further than making a young unfortunate feel a welcome guest. He showed her, through his actions, that we are indeed all part of God's family. And he instilled in his daughter a firm conviction to carry on his values: "My dad died last May and at his funeral everyone remembered him for his genuine love, care, and concern. . . . His love for others and having caring relationships is the value I treasure most. I pray the Lord will give me the grace to carry on those values and instill them in my children."

I was reminded of these qualities when I read a column by Jack Smith of the Los Angeles *Times*. He recently wrote that a nation's values can be inferred from the aspirations of its children. He cited an insightful study by a Los Angeles school teacher who asked her students to describe what they wanted to be when they grew up. The list from this class of twenty-one students was encouraging for those of us who ever doubted the future character development of our young. Almost half of the kids aspire to occupations in which they can help others, really a way of expressing love for others. Five want to be doctors, three want to be teachers. One wants to be a policeman, and another wants to be a fireman.

"Perhaps you will be as heartened as I," one parent said, "to learn that today's children are thinking about becoming something other than a Ninja Turtle."

I realize that one classroom can't speak for an entire nation of young people, but I've seen other examples that suggest the future is entrusted to a compassionate generation. One of the best illustrations of this was demonstrated in the lives of Joe White and his family who own and operate a series of Christian sports camps in Branson, Missouri.

One night Joe discussed with us his plans to complete construction of a special camp for handicapped and inner-city kids. The multi-million dollar facility was scheduled to open soon, and more than two thousand underprivileged children would benefit from it every summer for years to come.

An undertaking of this magnitude would not have been possible without many contributions from those who shared a vision for it. But I was overwhelmed to learn that one of the most generous benefactors to this project was Joe's fifteen-year-old daughter Jamie.

Don't love people so they
will love you,
love them because they
need to be loved.

Her amazing story began a few years earlier with an idea to launch her own clothing company and donate her profits to help build the special camp. Jamie's concept was to create outfits that were designed with the art found on commonplace flour sacks. The plan was full of risks. They had no sales force, no seamstresses, no materials, and no experience. Armed only with an idea (and a bizarre one at that) and a burden to reach underprivileged kids, the White family invested their savings in the project. Only God could have brought about what followed. Against incredible odds, Jamie's business flourished and generated almost $600,000 in sales during the first two years of operation.

When asked about her charity, Jamie responded, "I'm no saint. I'm just glad God chose to put me in a position where I'm able to help." Jamie has learned the meaning and the true rewards of helping—and loving—others. One of my readers wrote about her motivation to be compassionate: "Don't love people so they will love you, love them because they need to be loved. If you do that, you'll find you have more friends than you can count."

The lesson of giving runs deep. One woman enumerated a long list of things her parents did for others—from visiting shut-ins to tutoring to sewing for disadvantaged children. Their examples served well, she went on to say, even though they weren't Christians! She ended her letter with this call to action: "You cannot simply talk about feeding the hungry, housing the homeless, and caring for the ill. You must put action into words."

These letters and Jamie's spirit remind me of the selfless attitude that seemed so characteristic of previous generations. This longstanding heritage of selflessness was emphasized to me recently when I saw Ken Burns' epic series on the Civil War. Again and again the historians involved in the project spoke of the sacrifices made by people who subjugated their own interests for the sake of others. One of the most moving letters read against a panorama of photographs from the war years was that of Major Sullivan Ballou of Rhode Island. He wrote to his wife, Sarah, on the eve of the first battle of Bull Run:

I have no misgivings about or lack of confidence in the cause in which I am engaged and my courage does not halt or falter. I know how American civilization now leans upon the triumph of the government and how great a debt we owe to those who went before us through the blood and suffering of the Revolution. And I am willing, perfectly willing to lay down all my joys in this life to help maintain this government and to pay that debt.

Sarah, my love for you is deathless. It seems to bind me with mighty cables that nothing but Omnipotence can break. And yet my love of country comes over me like a strong wind and bears me irresistibly with all those chains to the battlefield. The memory of all the blissful moments I have enjoyed with you come crowding over me and I feel most deeply grateful to God and you that I have enjoyed them for so long. And how hard it is for me to give them up and burn to ashes the hopes and future years, when God willing, we still might have lived and loved together, and seen our boys grown up to honorable manhood around us. If I do not return, my dear Sarah, never forget how much I loved you nor that when my last breath escapes me on the battlefield it will whisper your name.

One week later, Major Ballou was killed at Bull Run. Although he perished in the early months of the Civil War, his letter has endured for more than a century as a testimony to his selfless convictions.

This same sense of personal sacrifice was captured in the popular musical *Les Misérables*. In one scene, Marius, a young revolutionary is torn between his desire to fight and his desire to run away with his new love, Cosette. As he

explains his torment, he is suddenly upbraided by one of his compatriots:

Marius, you're no longer a child
I do not doubt you mean it well
But now there is a higher call.
Who cares about your lonely soul?
We strive towards a larger goal.
Our little lives don't count at all!

While these words are harsh, the concept here is that our lives are indeed insignificant when we pursue our own interests. But we gain meaning and purpose when we submit ourselves to a bigger cause. That's the lesson Jamie White and her contemporaries have already learned so well. Their compassion today offers tremendous hope for tomorrow.

Ultimately we must also teach our young that the cause of Christ is where they can find the greatest significance. It is there, in his army, where they will find true fulfillment and can help others in this life and for eternity. But how do we teach this principle to our children? Every parent must be on the lookout for the teachable moments.

A friend told me of an encouraging *and* disconcerting experience he had while tucking his children in bed for the night. As he prepared to pray with his eleven-year-old son, they also had their routine discussion of the day's events. The young boy was obviously troubled about something. After some gentle prodding, he shared what was on his heart.

"Dad, there's a kid in my class who has no friends because everybody thinks he is different. They call him bad names and they won't let him play with them."

"What are you going to do about it?" the father asked.

"I've decided to be his friend—even if the other kids won't like me for doing it."

My friend's heart swelled with pride. His

Our lives are indeed insignificant when we pursue our own interests.

---

son was taking a stand on behalf of a less-fortunate child and this compassion was no doubt a result of his own successful parental influence. But that pride was quickly dispelled in the next few moments when he had a remark-

ably similar, yet very different conversation with his nine-year-old daughter in the next room.

As he knelt down at her bedside, he inquired about her day.

"Well, Dad, there is this strange girl in our class, and all the kids make fun of her."

"Oh," responded the proud father. "I'll bet you've decided to become her friend."

"No way!" the daughter exclaimed. "She is *so* weird and I don't want anything to do with her."

How could two siblings raised under the same roof have such different reactions to similar situations? One possessed the warm heart of a missionary while the other had the cold shoulder of a stock broker. How could one be inclined toward compassion while the other was indifferent? These perplexing questions plagued my friend. And, of course, his nine-year-old daughter had in *not* showing compassion presented my friend with a "teachable moment," an opportunity to talk with her about Jesus' love for all people and his wish that we follow suit.

Perhaps the Apostle Paul offered a meaningful answer in his letter to the Romans. "We have different gifts according to the grace given us. If a man's gift is . . . contributing to the needs of others, let him give generously" (Romans 12:6, 8).

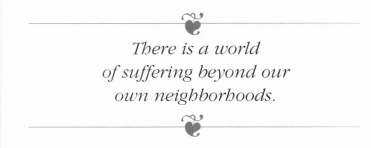

There is a world of suffering beyond our own neighborhoods.

Paul seems to be saying that some people are naturally or spiritually endowed with certain qualities like compassion. As parents, we should encourage our children to develop and fully employ those spiritual gifts. While we can take some comfort in knowing that all our children aren't expected to be like Mother Teresa, we also realize that Jesus' second greatest commandment was to "Love your neighbor as yourself" (Matthew 22:39).

We can also teach our sons and daughters that there is a world of suffering beyond our own neighborhoods. Unfortunately, our kids won't get a reliable perspective of this plight through the media. In 1988, for example, the press sent an army of reporters to cover the story of three trapped whales in Alaska. Several

governments cooperated to rescue these animals, and the media heralded this account to inquiring minds around the world. Sadly, the same year, more than a quarter of a million people died of starvation in the Sudan. Their terrible tragedy never made the front page.

In fact, more children die in the Third World every two days than all the American servicemen killed in the Vietnam War. In some countries like Tanzania, one out of five children will die before the age of five from diseases such as measles, malnourishment, diarrhea, and malaria. This is the stark reality of life and death in the Southern Hemisphere.

Our own offspring must learn they have a duty to share their abundance with those who are born, through no fault of their own, into horrible poverty. Relief organizations like World Vision in Monrovia, California, offer an excellent vehicle to teach our children to practice compassion and experience its rich rewards. Our family has "adopted" two youngsters through World Vision's sponsorship program, and they have now become a part of our extended family.

Of course, there are other ways to model kindness to our children. One woman who responded to our survey shared how her father made an impact on her in this regard when she was young.

"One night my dad was returning home from a business trip," she said. "At the airport he

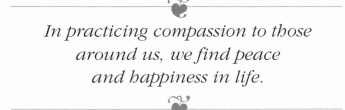

In practicing compassion to those around us, we find peace and happiness in life.

observed an older couple who apparently needed some assistance. He learned they were traveling from Estonia to Canada and had a layover in our city. They only had a few dollars in their pockets and had no idea where to go. So my dad invited these bewildered strangers to our home for dinner and to spend the night. The next morning, he took them back to the airport and helped them catch their connecting flight.

"You can imagine how instances like these taught me the value of being kind. Today, I attribute my compassionate tendencies to the behavior I observed in my father," she said.

Dr. James Dobson was once asked, "What one feature should be changed in Western culture in order to produce a higher percentage of

emotionally healthy children and adults?" His response was very revealing.

"From my perspective," the psychologist said, "the most valuable revision would be for adults to begin actively teaching children to love and respect one another (and, of course, for these adults to demonstrate that love in their own lives)."

Dr. Dobson found in his experience as a counselor that most emotional problems can be traced to one of two places (or both): either from an unloving or unnourishing relationship with parents, or from an inability to gain acceptance and respect from peers.

Thus, when Jesus commanded us to love others as ourselves, he was offering us the key to self-preservation. In practicing compassion to those around us, we find peace and happiness in life. That is an important piece of advice for parents.

While our children may not naturally possess the spiritual gift of compassion, we can give them one of life's greatest rewards by teaching them to love others.

S

erve him in sincerity
and in truth.

Joshua 24:14

Honesty Begins At Home

I was having dinner with a friend a few years ago when our conversation turned to the subject of how our children can teach significant principles to us. My friend then told me of an experience he had in this regard.

One evening his teenage daughter asked his permission to watch the nighttime soap opera "Dynasty." Although my friend had never seen the program, he knew of its reputation. "I don't think it's the type of program we ought to watch," he told her.

"But Dad, all the kids at school are talking about it," came the predictable reply.

My friend relented on the condition that he would view it with her. He was shocked at what he saw that night.

"The characters were involved in adultery, homosexuality, deceit, cheating, vanity, and greed," he told me. "I felt that I had dishonored God by allowing this program in my home. I just hoped that the incident would pass by and be forgotten."

But one week later, my friend's daughter approached him with the same request. "Can we watch it one more time, Dad?"

Perhaps it will be better this time. I'll give it one more chance, my friend thought.

Of course, there was no improvement, and within a few minutes my friend stood up and

said, "Honey, I cannot watch this program. Everything that I stand for is being assaulted here. It violates my conscience. I'm going to another room, and I just pray that the Lord will speak to you about this."

Children notice when we say one thing and do another, even if we do so with the best of intentions.

Before he could turn away, his daughter responded. "Daddy, I thought that you would have said this last week. I've just been waiting for you to take a stand. I really don't care about this program."

Talk about practical faith! My friend suddenly realized that his daughter was watching him more than she was watching the program. She had been using "Dynasty" to test the honesty and validity of the values he had been teaching her since she was young.

Integrity is consistent and congruent. Children notice when we say one thing and do another, even if we do so with the best of in-

tentions. Like so many other values explored in this book, honesty is best taught by example, so our children can catch it.

Chuck Swindoll, in his book, *The Quest for Character,* developed this point: "Ideally, we plant the seeds and cultivate the roots of honesty in the home. Under the watchful eyes of consistent, diligent, persistent parents! In the best laboratory of life God ever designed—the family unit. It is *there* a proper scale of values is imbibed as the worth of a dollar is learned. It is on that anvil that the appreciation for hard work, the esteem for truth, the reward for achievement, and the cost of dishonesty are hammered out so that a life is shaped correctly down deep inside."

Yes. Integrity starts at home, and it then extends around the neighborhood, onto the playing field, and to the school. One woman who responded to our survey said that this character value was emphasized so strongly by her parents that it placed her in an unusual predicament.

"The second cardinal rule in our family was honesty," she wrote. "I remember one occasion during a fourth-grade spelling quiz when *I* was put to the test. The teacher pronounced the word 'Christmas' and asked us to spell it. The

class began to giggle with glee because the same word was written in bold letters on the bulletin board behind her. But I was so determined not be a cheater that I averted my eyes and *purposely* misspelled the word!"

What a different world this would be if we had more adults who had that kind of character. Sadly, the evidence that there aren't surrounds us. Politicians betray their constituents. Stock brokers rip off their clients. Savings and loan executives live high on the hog while squandering their depositors' life savings.

One of my readers may have had this in mind when he wrote, "Integrity is more valuable than money; it can't be bought for any amount, and, once relinquished, can't be repurchased."

Ideally, we plant the seeds and cultivate the roots of honesty in the home.

When I was a college student, my journalism professors repeatedly reminded me that a reporter should always be objective and fair when covering the news. Before I ever received my diploma, however, that lesson was quickly undermined by the political realities of life.

On the school newspaper, I reported that one of the departmental deans on campus had confidentially instructed his faculty to manipulate their pupils' grades. This dean, known as a disciplinarian, complained that too many students were receiving A's. He wanted to see more C's. As you can imagine, the story created quite an uproar, and the university administration reversed the policy.

I thought I had performed a credible service to the academic community, but I was reprimanded by my faculty adviser. "How could you do this to Joe?" he asked. "He's my best friend and golfing buddy! He'll probably lose a promotion over this." So much for objectivity. Unbiased reporting was a terrific theory in the classroom, but it went out the window when it affected golfing buddies.

Since then, I have heard professional journalists admit that pure objectivity is an unattainable goal—so they use their news reports as platforms for their own particular viewpoints. Richard G. Capen, Jr., vice-chairman of the Knight-Ridder, Inc., newspaper chain has found that our entire society has been affected by ethical shortcomings. He commented on our reactions to the dishonesty all around us. "Banks delay clearing checks because they don't trust their customers," he said. "Hospital emergency rooms turn away patients because they fear they won't be paid. We install burglar alarms, carry guns, insist on prenuptial agreements and employment contracts because no one trusts anyone anymore."

As parents we need to be examples of righteousness to our sons and daughters and to teach them that God will honor them for truthfulness.

That sad commentary was reinforced by a book entitled *The Day America Told the Truth*. People "lie at the drop of a hat. Lying is part of their lives," says co-author James Patterson, chairman of the J. Walter Thompson advertising agency. He reported that 91 percent of Americans say they lie routinely, and 36 percent of those confess to dark, important lies that hurt others.

No wonder parents who responded to our survey placed honesty as the third most important value to teach our children. One wise mother tried to teach integrity to her kids by assuring them that if they admitted a wrong, she would not punish them. In so doing, she eliminated her children's fear of being punished for telling the truth. She gave her children the gift of being able to admit their mistakes honestly, a gift beyond price.

This reminds me of the immigrant family who came to America and tried to adopt their new country's ways. They heard the familiar fable of young George Washington mischievously chopping down a cherry tree. When confronted by his dad, George said, "Father, I cannot tell a lie." As a result of his honesty, the lad escaped punishment.

The immigrant's son remembered this story when he was justly accused of tipping over an outhouse as a prank. "Father, like the famous American, George Washington, I cannot tell a lie. I pushed the outhouse over." Immediately upon making this confession, the boy received a terrible spanking from his dad. When he had stopped sobbing and had wiped his tears away, the young immigrant expressed his confusion to his father. "George Washington wasn't punished when he told the truth!"

"Ah yes, son. But George Washington's father was not in the cherry tree."

Our children need to learn the consequences of dishonesty as well as the rewards for integrity. The Proverbs of Solomon tell us that "even a child is known by his actions, by whether his conduct is pure and right" (Proverbs 20:11). As parents we need to be examples of righteousness to our sons and daughters and to teach them that God will honor them for truthfulness. The building blocks of character described in this book are stacked on a foundation of honesty—and that value begins at home.

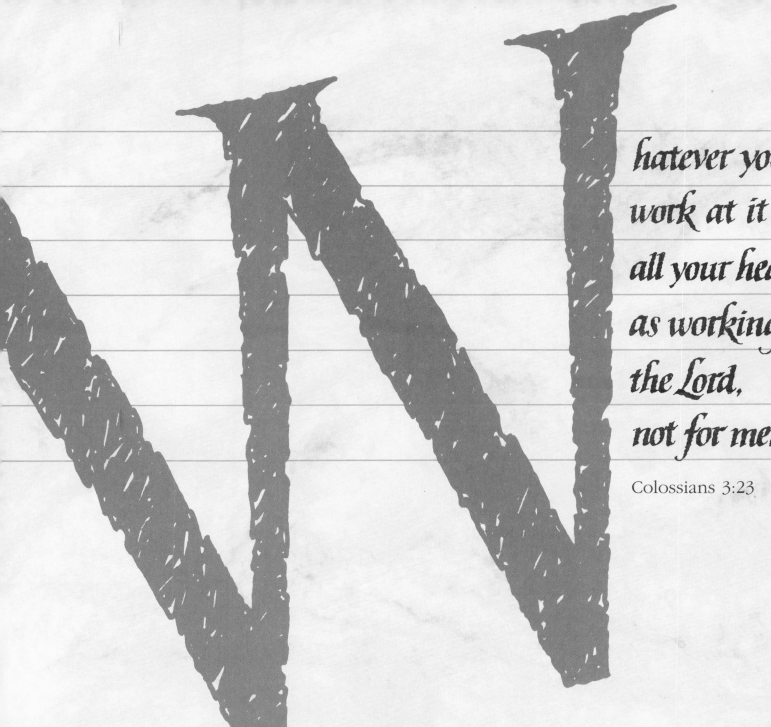

hatever you do,
work at it with
all your heart,
as working for
the Lord,
not for men.

Colossians 3:23

Where There's A Will, There's Work

As I read through the stacks of letters from parents whose opinions helped shape this book, I was surprised to learn how much they wanted to teach their children healthy attitudes about work. Of course, they wanted their kids to do better with homework, cleaning their rooms, and practicing the piano, but the concerns I read from these mothers and fathers went far deeper and dealt with more significant issues.

Many parents today want to lay a groundwork of values about work that will help their children lead productive lives through adulthood. Perhaps these concerns result from the schizophrenic view of work they see operating in society today.

On the one hand, we have become a nation of workaholics. *Psychology Today* magazine reported: "Work has become our intoxicant, and Americans are working harder than ever before. In the past fifteen years, the typical adult's leisure time has shrunk by 40 percent. And the work week, after decades of getting shorter, is suddenly 15 percent longer." Undoubtedly, there are many moms and dads caught in this cycle who want their offspring to lead productive lives that are balanced between work and recreation.

On the other hand, parents are also concerned about the deteriorating work ethic and how it will affect their children. Our society, which was built on dedication, diligence, and disciplined labor, is now riddled with problems by those who cheat, steal, and compromise. The headlines are filled with the names of former financial personalities like Ivan Boesky, Michael Milkin, and Leona Helmsley, who amassed huge fortunes at the expense and devastation of others. One revealing fact about sagging ethics comes from retail stores which report that employee theft, not shoplifting, is the major cause of shrinkage. Other unfortunate examples are provided by those companies that knowingly put the public at danger by electing to use inferior materials in their machinery. Meanwhile, the welfare system now supports the third successive generation in many families who have grown accustomed to depending on others.

For all these reasons and more, parents listed the value of hard work as the fourth most significant principle to pass along. As I read their letters, I was able to define four basic attitudes that mothers and fathers want their children to embrace:

1. Be industrious.

In the summer of 1990, our family had a wonderful vacation in the Ozark mountains near Branson, Missouri. A friend loaned us his cabin, and for several days we enjoyed water skiing, fishing, reading, eating, and plenty of resting. It was a tremendous break from the harried pace of our normal routines.

A few days into our holiday, we were joined by my parents who flew in from California. This vacation was going to be a good respite for them as well. They are simply the hardest working people I know, and they deserved a little relaxation. For as long as I can remember, Dad has held two jobs at the same time. He works all day long as an administrator for the local school district, comes home for dinner, and then dashes off to night school where he teaches immigrants to speak English. Mom has also had dual careers. In addition to her household responsibilities, she has worked at a department store where she deals with customer complaints among other things. They always seemed to have an inexhaustible supply of energy, but I figured a week in the Ozarks was going to be therapeutic for them.

The morning after their arrival, I woke at seven o'clock and noticed that the stillness of the Missouri mountains was broken by the sounds of hustle and bustle. I rose from my bed and walked to the front door where I saw a scene that came as no surprise.

My folks were working away like a downtown construction crew. Dad had found a broom and was vigorously sweeping the front porch. Mom was kneeling in the flower bed attacking the weeds. The sprinkler was going full blast, providing water to a dry spot on the lawn. My folks had arrived, bringing their bottled energy on vacation. There was work to be done, and they were taking care of it!

I know it must sound like they are obsessed with labor, but I have always admired their willingness to throw themselves fully into any task. And during this vacation, in which they had plenty of relaxation, they had the fun and reward of doing a different kind of work—and of leaving the cabin nicer than they found it. Their examples have taught and motivated me to be a busy person. When I was a child, I was encouraged to seek odd jobs throughout the neighborhood. Pulling weeds, mowing lawns, washing cars, and collecting bottles were my industries. When I was in junior high school I became an aggressive paperboy. One summer, a friend and I persuaded the local newspaper to assign five routes to us, and for three months we worked like dogs to deliver the morning edition before our customers went to work. When I was a college student, I

learned that I did my best work when I carried the heaviest academic load and had a job on the side. I could never understand the prevailing philosophy about life that was summarized by John Lennon who sang "Let It Be." Fortunately, that laissez-faire attitude has been replaced today by slogans that say "Just Do It" and "Make It Happen."

I encourage parents to allow their children plenty of playtime. But it is equally important that we teach our children to be productive people who contribute to their own improvement and the improvement of the world around them.

2. Don't quit. All of us can remember our first job out of school. Like drinking coffee, it was a part of the passage to adulthood. We'll never try as hard to succeed in a position as we did in that initial flight into the work-a-day world. Unfortunately, these early attempts do not always meet with tremendous success.

I remember one friend who was hired right out of college by a local television station to be their off-camera announcer. His assignment was simply to read the station's call letters every half-hour between programs. His broadcast debut was scheduled for three o'clock one

afternoon. Filled with excitement and pride, he spent the morning of his first day calling friends and relatives to remind them of his big moment.

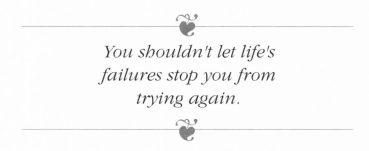

You shouldn't let life's failures stop you from trying again.

In the final hour before his premier, he went to the men's room (he didn't have an office) where he rehearsed his lines. With a black marker, he wrote variations of his script on a piece of cardboard and then practiced them repeatedly in his sonorous voice: "KOMO—4 Seattle . . . 4 Seattle—This is KOMO . . . KOMO—Channel 4."

Finally, the time came. He took his seat in the announcer's booth and waited for the engineer's cue. He watched the second hand sweep toward destiny. At exactly 3:00 P.M., the engineer flicked a switch and pointed at him.

Sometimes three seconds can last an eternity, and that's what my friend remembers most about that day. He opened his mouth to speak the words he had rehearsed so well. But, for three agonizing ticks of the clock, he managed to sputter only one letter—over and over: "K-K-K-K-K."

When he looked up, the engineer's face was in his hands and my friend imagined that the whole world was laughing hysterically. At that point, I'm sure he was tempted to become a faceless bum and catch a freight train to nowhere in particular. But something within his character caused him to pull himself up by his bootstraps and try again. Today my friend owns a thriving media consulting agency. As he looks back on that painful experience he says, "It was a setback. But I learned as a child that you shouldn't let life's failures stop you from trying again."

Our children will succeed in life if they heed this advice because failures are inevitable. One night I took my daughter on a date to the local frozen yogurt shop. In the car she revealed something that had been deeply troubling her. "Dad, I've been trying out for the fifth-grade track team, and I don't think I'm going to make it. The coach is only going to use the top five girls in competition."

She was so discouraged. At that moment I had two choices. I could blame the coach, complain about an unfair system, and tell her

that she was being mistreated. Or I could face the situation squarely and help Viveca understand that life is characterized by peaks and valleys, wins and losses, victories and failures. I chose the latter and explained that she should continue to participate in the workouts, even if she felt the odds were against her. (I didn't tell her that with our family's gene pool, she didn't stand a chance!) We acknowledged the pain of this possible defeat, but we put it in its proper perspective. Most importantly, I wanted Viveca to understand that perseverance had its own rewards. Even though it seemed inevitable that she would be cut from the team, I urged her to continue her training right to the end.

Life is characterized by peaks and valleys, wins and losses, victories and failures.

A few days later, the coach called the girls together on the track and read the list of the final five. Viveca's name was not included. It was tough for her, and she could have avoided the humiliation if she had quit early. As a result of this ordeal, a building block of character was added to the structure of her life. Someday, when the stakes are much higher, I believe she will have a foundation to deal adequately with the setbacks that are unavoidable in human experience.

3. Do your best. I am often asked why Focus on the Family has grown so dramatically over the past decade. When I joined the staff in 1981, there were 30 people working in cramped offices in Arcadia, California. The radio program was heard on 200 radio stations, and a monthly newsletter was mailed to 35,000 supporters. The next year this small ministry doubled in size. It doubled the next year and the next. Today, more than 700 staff are employed by this media and counseling ministry which reaches millions of people over a network of 1,450 stations, and 7 magazines are published and circulated to more than 2 million homes every month. The outreach includes videos, films, and books in North America and in several countries overseas.

Why has this explosive growth occurred in such a relatively short period of time? Apart from the obvious answer of God's blessing, a major reason has been our staff's unqualified commitment to excellence. When we produce a radio program, it reflects Dr. Dobson's best efforts. And he is supported by a team of professionals who share his passion for quality.

The Bible tells us that even God is pleased by those who give it their all.

I believe the public has responded to Focus on the Family because the advice it offers is sound and it is presented in a first-class fashion.

Not long ago I received a call from one of the national television networks. They had seen our "McGee and Me" video series and were interested in discussing how they could use it. When I arrived at the network headquarters, I was ushered into the office of the children's programming manager. Producers all over Hollywood would kill for the opportunity to meet with this woman.

I sat down on the couch opposite her desk and she got right to the point. "Someone sent me this video," she said as she waved a "McGee and Me" tape. "So one day while I was having lunch in my office, I put it in the machine. I figured it was going to be just another mediocre production because I had never heard of you guys. But I was amazed. It is a great script and the production quality is superb. Even more importantly, you and your associates have done something we've never been able to do at the network. You've been able to teach values without being corny."

Even Hollywood respects a traditional message when it is done right. I've seen this principle applied in the business community also. I recently had dinner with Orville Merillat, founder and namesake of the huge cabinet and furniture manufacturer in Adrian, Michigan. When I asked him his key to success, he responded, "Always do your best—and then do some more."

The Bible tells us that even God is pleased by those who give it their all. The Old Testament Scriptures reveal that he was particularly happy with Caleb, who attacked every assignment "wholeheartedly" (Joshua 14:8, 9, 14). Whether he was sent on a reconnaissance or engaged in battle, Caleb always gave it his best shot.

Let us, as parents, teach our kids to reach for the highest grades in the classroom and for first place on the athletic field. It's not important that they finish number one, only that they push themselves to the limits of the skills and wisdom God has granted them.

4. *Pay your dues.* Our children are growing up in a high-tech society where lasers, scanners, computers, fax machines, and microwave ovens provide instantaneous results. We all take these marvelous conveniences for granted, but I wonder if our children will expect their personal rewards to come as quickly as signals ricochet off satellites.

Even if they apply the three aforementioned principles, they need to know that there is still no guarantee of success. Be industrious. Don't quit. Do your best. Just add water and serve. It only takes a minute.

No, that's not enough. There is still one more ingredient for developing a healthy attitude about work, and it's called "Paying your dues." I would like to share a story by Dr. Dobson that illustrates this point.

On a trip to Washington, D.C., a few years ago, my hotel room was located next to the room of a famous cellist who was in the city to give a classical concert that evening. I could hear him through the walls as he practiced hour after hour. He did not play beautiful symphonic renditions; he repeated scales and runs and exercises, over and over and over.

This practice began early in the morning (believe me!) and continued until the time of his concert. As he strolled on stage that evening, I'm sure many individuals in the audience thought to themselves, What a glamorous life! Some glamour! I happen to know that he had spent the entire day in his lonely hotel room in the company of his cello.

It has been interesting for me to observe how many people make the same false assumption about Dr. Dobson. Aspiring counselors and psychologists have called Al Sanders, president of the agency which represents the Focus on the Family radio program. "I would like to host my own radio program," they say. "I think I could be the next James Dobson."

Oh, if it were only that easy! These idealistic folks have no idea how long and hard Dr. Dobson has worked to develop the style and polish that seemingly come so easy for him. In my previous biography about him, *Dr. Dobson: Turning Hearts Toward Home,* I described how he spoke and wrote in relative obscurity for many years.

Like the cellist and any other accomplished professional, Dr. Dobson's success was paid for with the dues of sweat and toil. Authors have a favorite expression that describes the situation, "Everyone likes to have written, but no one likes to write."

When I was a child taking piano lessons, my dad used a system that helped me practice my repetitions. He placed a bundle of match sticks on one end of the keyboard. Every time I played a particular piece, I could move one stick to the other end. By the time all the sticks were piled together again, I knew I had learned that piece of music.

The stories people shared about learning the value of hard work almost glow with the warmth and love in their memories. One woman wrote, "My parents taught me the value of work. Nobody owed me anything. I wanted a new bike, which was fine as long as I paid for it. So I spent a whole summer collecting newspapers and aluminum to raise enough money. Dad was always willing to help me earn money from junk, tag sales, flea markets, or odd jobs, but I had to work. I still laugh about the time we brought a truckload of old cast-iron radiators to the junk man, who told me not to help get them off the truck because he didn't want me to hurt myself. Dad asked him who he thought helped get them on the truck."

One man started his anecdote about working hard with these words, "My father's efforts to better his life are a legend in our family." He goes on to tell the story of his father, the son of sharecroppers, who took correspondence courses so he could get a better job that would also allow him to spend more time with his family. He closes by saying, "It's uncanny how closely my life parallels my father's, and I often thank the good Lord for giving me such a great example to follow."

As our kids approach adulthood, I believe it is important for us to help them understand that our most precious achievements are those purchased with our greatest efforts.

Remember the Lord who is great and awesome, and fight for your brothers, your sons and your daughters, your wives and your homes.

Nehemiah 4:14

SIX

Commitment To The Family

I know a place created by God as part of his plan for our existence and survival. I know a place where I am loved and accepted. I know a place where I am forgiven when I make a mistake. I know a place where I belong. This place is called the family.

In response to my survey on values, we received many letters from parents who want to teach their children about the many attributes of family life. They outlined several significant points.

First, the family is where we receive our identity. As one who bears an unusual name, I have always been sensitive about the significance an appellation can have. My Swedish parents chose not to give me an All-American name, and so I have become a little philosophical about the importance of titles. It seems like I am continually engaged in conversations with people who want to know how to pronounce my name, what it means, what did my parents have in mind when they gave it to me, and "Is it German?"

My name seems simple enough to me, but it apparently is quite an obstacle for those who can't read phonetically. For example, my first name is Rolf. Now to any person who can read and pronounce the word "golf," my name should not present any formidable challenge.

Yet, I have learned to turn my head when people say, "Roff," "Rofe," "Rulf," or just plain "Ralph."

Never give up on kids.
God is faithful!

My family shares the same experience regarding our surname. The letters that spell Zettersten appear to form three simple syllables, but we've all been hailed "Zettersteen," "Zetterstine," "Zetterson," or even "Zerstein."

Put all those loose translations together and you can see the potential for catastrophe. Rolf Zettersten becomes Roff Zerstein. Please don't feel sorry for me. Like the boy named Sue, I have developed a tough hide, and my self-esteem is never affected by those who ruthlessly butcher it or ask intrusive questions as though I were the Elephant man.

Furthermore, I learned the virtue of patience at an early age because all of my schoolteachers thought the best way to take roll call, to return assignments, or to distribute anything of value was in alphabetical order. (Someday, "the last shall be first." Amen.)

While our society does not place any importance on names, it is interesting to note other cultures that do. The Israelites, as described throughout the Bible, put great emphasis on names. It was typical for them to make their offspring living testimonials of godly characteristics by giving them meaningful names. For example, Hezekiah means "Jehovah strengthens," Amos means "burden-bearer," Mathias means "gift of God," and Zechariah means "Jehovah remembers."

Author Paul Tournier suggests that a parent can actually help shape the character of a child by selecting a name which has significant meaning. A name is much more than a label, he says, it is definitive.

There is great authority granted to a parent in being allowed to name another human being. When God gave Adam dominion over the earth, he also granted him the power to name every living creature. The two responsibilities went hand in hand and every parent must take these seriously.

We know who we are by knowing who we're related to. One of my friends recalled that as a child he was repeatedly told: "No matter what happens, you are a Smith." What does this say to a youngster? It says, "You belong somewhere—even if you blow it." This leads us to a second attribute of the committed family.

Jesus' message in the beautiful imagery of the parable of the Prodigal Son speaks about the concept of forgiveness. The wayward child knew he would be accepted at home. And he wasn't just accepted, he was welcomed like royalty into his own home, his own family.

One young man wrote about his story as a modern-day prodigal. One of his top three important values was "Never give up on your kids." He went on to say, "I gave my parents more reason to give up on me than most. I was from a middle-class family, and I was involved in alcohol, drugs, and wild parties. My dad paid fines and bails for me. I was arrested for dealing drugs and given two years in prison. I accepted Christ while in prison, and God has not stopped blessing me since. My parents' faith never wavered. Never give up on kids. God is faithful!"

A young woman wrote about her prodigal experience. "When I married against my parents' advice I literally alienated myself from my family. I never made an effort to see them. All attempts to keep communication open between us were made by my parents. Within two years the marriage was over, and I felt like a failure.

My parents never condemned me, never said 'I told you so.'" Her letter continues, "At my sister's wedding I started to feel like a failure all over again, even though I had rebuilt my life. After my sister left, I went into the nursery of the church where I could be by myself and cry. I guess Dad must have sensed my mood, because he knocked and came in. He never spoke a word, but he held me in his arms and let me cry as long as I wanted to. I asked him, 'Dad, am I okay?' He answered, 'You are so special to me and I love you. I never stopped loving you.'

True love says: I will love you regardless of what you do to me, how you act toward me, or what you think of me.

"True love says: I will love you regardless of what you do to me, how you act toward me, or what you think of me. I have seen this kind of sacrificial love in my parents, and now I strive to model it in my own life."

A third virtue of the family pertains to the celebration that occurs there. Your family is the

group of people who not only embrace you in defeat, they also honor you in victory. As parents, we must teach our kids that their family, their mom, their dad, their sister, their brother are the best in the world.

Fourth, the family is a laboratory where scriptural principles are tested under all conditions. One woman wrote about how she wanted to model values for her children: "Affirm and encourage children often, criticize seldom; do not be afraid to discipline (yes, even spank!); apologize openly to children when you're wrong; expect respect (which children give if parents earn it); let the children know they are trusted; keep communication channels open; and set godly examples." This is a good and comprehensive to-do list to live by as parents.

Knowing that our values are being tested within the close confines of the family, we must be sensitive to the little ones who are watching us. A few weeks ago, my daughter, Viveca, accompanied me to a department store where I picked up a suit that had been altered. I tried it on, and the tailor pronounced it a good fit. I nodded approvingly as I turned from side to side in front of the mirror.

But a tug from my young daughter set me

straight. "Dad, the sleeves aren't even," she whispered. Viveca was right, of course.

Not much escapes the intense gaze of a child, and lately my wife, Linda, and I have been reexamining the input our kids receive from a number of sources. We do a pretty good job of screening the television programs they watch and the radio stations they hear. But a recent incident reminded us of another critical area we must monitor carefully.

Not long ago, our son, Peter, was invited to spend the night at a friend's house. We granted permission because we knew his pal

---

The family is a laboratory where scriptural principles are tested under all conditions.

---

was a good student and the parents were decent folks. But after Peter returned home the next morning, we learned that his friend's older teenage brothers had spent the evening playing an occult fantasy game with violent themes.

Nothing terrible happened that night, but the incident made us aware of the need for some ground rules regarding sleepovers. Why? Because many parents don't share our value system. This can be confusing to children who become accustomed to one moral code but suddenly find themselves in an environment that operates by a completely different standard. To this end, we recognize that our family's values are not always shared by others, and we must protect our children from contradictory situations.

I don't know if my kids will eventually grow up to be blindly and happily oblivious of those pressures that quietly undermine my values, but right now they are observing everything and soaking it all in. As a child, I learned the Sunday school chorus, "Be careful little eyes what you see. Be careful little ears what you hear."

As a parent, I can help my children heed this warning by avoiding situations and environments that contradict the values I want them to learn during this impressionable period of their lives. Even after our children have grown up and left home, they will feel the effects of belonging to a family. Two men wrote letters about this. The first said, "I'm thirty-eight years old, and my parents are still concerned about me and nearly every facet of my life—

mental, physical, financial, and, most of all, spiritual."

Another sent me a long thank-you letter he had recently sent to his own parents. He began

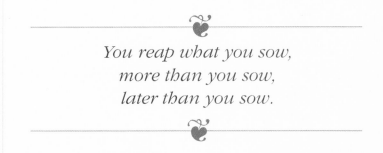

You reap what you sow,
more than you sow,
later than you sow.

with thanking his dad for teaching him to respect and honor his wife: "Even as a teenage husband in trying circumstances, I knew, by your example, that my wife was to be my best friend, closest adviser, and most faithful advocate and that I should cherish her with all my strength. I cringe when I see the way some men treat their wives as their sons and daughters watch and learn."

He thanks both his mother and father at length for what they've given him, their son, a member of their family. And then he quoted one of his own favorite Christian writers, Charles Stanley's paraphrase of the Bible, "You reap what you sow, more than you sow, later than you sow." In concluding, he assured his parents that he didn't intend to keep the love and values they'd given him to himself, but that he would do all he could to pass them along to his children.

One woman shared this profound thought about family: "My parents' lives were committed to Jesus Christ. They were not perfect Christians. They didn't demand spiritual, superficial perfection from their children. Instead they focused on the character within—the deceitful, dishonest, and selfish heart needed to be changed by God into a heart of teachability, integrity, and kindness."

Finally, let me suggest another purpose for the family. It is the first place for evangelism. As parents, we all learn to be evangelists and prayer warriors for the sake of the little ones entrusted to us by God. Therein lies the ultimate objective for the family—to nurture precious souls into God's kingdom.

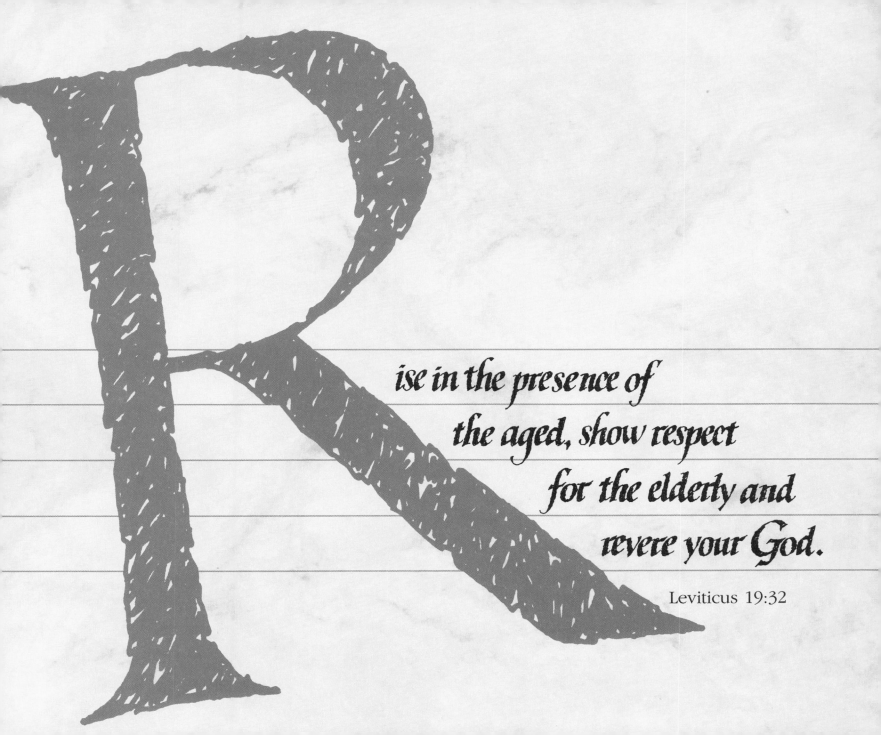

Rise in the presence of the aged, show respect for the elderly and revere your God.

Leviticus 19:32

Respect Your Elders

My friend, John Eckhardt, operates one of the finest dude ranches in North America. In a beautiful place nestled along the Smith River in Montana, his guests spend their days riding horses over rugged hills and across lush valleys. One of the highlights of this ranch is the tremendous service and attention these guests receive. An army of young people serve as waiters, ranch hands, maids, drivers, and even babysitters.

Every winter John travels a circuit of colleges in the Southern states where he recruits his summer staff. When I asked why he goes so far to find help, his response startled me: "Because that's the only part of the country where I can find young people who haven't forgotten their 'Yes Ma'ams' and 'Yes Sirs,'" he said.

When I was young, I was taught never to address adults by their first names. My parents felt it was important for me to show respect by this formality. I realize that our society is more casual today, and I enjoy many aspects of that. But one problem with that approach to life is the declining honor and respect we show for our elders.

Apparently, many other parents share this feeling because it was reflected throughout the letters from those who replied to our survey. Several people used this opportunity to express appreciation for their own parents.

A man in his sixties wrote about the numerous lessons about respect his mother passed along to him: "I was taught to never belittle people because of their color, race, or circumstances. She reminded me that our circumstances were on the nether side of perfect. She instructed me to show respect for women as I'm sure God designed it. And she taught me to respect my elders."

This woman had lived a life of tremendous joys, great accomplishments, and deep sorrows.

Another woman shared her thoughts from her upbringing and how it has influenced her attitude toward seniors. "It is the duty and privilege of family members to care for their elderly and infirmed," she said. She continued to say that the values her parents taught were "more by example than pronouncement." That principle is truly reflected in the ending of her letter: "Mother is old now—eighty-seven. Her physical strength and her memory have failed considerably, but going to church is the highlight of her week. She 'drives me crazy' making sure she knows what day it is so she won't miss church. As if I would keep her away! I would feel just as empty if I missed. What a blessing she has been, and continues to be, in my life."

Showing respect and deference to the elderly is an important principle. Yet I feel we must go beyond that lesson when instructing our children. It is important that our kids learn to appreciate the intrinsic worth of senior citizens.

Not long ago, my wife and I rented the popular video *Driving Miss Daisy* to watch with our two older children. We suspected the movie might be too slow-paced for our rambunctious eleven- and fourteen-year-olds, but we wanted them to see it because it is a beautiful story that teaches an important principle.

Driving Miss Daisy is the story of a relationship between a rich elderly Jewish woman and her aging black chauffeur. In addition to being entertaining, this movie makes a powerful statement about the dignity of all human beings—regardless of race, religion, or age. Much to our delight, our kids were not only captivated by the drama, but they also captured the significant lessons it taught. Afterward we had a meaningful family discussion about the value of senior citizens as represented in the film.

The movie reminded me of my own early experiences with older people. When I was sixteen, I got my first job from a retired insurance executive who hired me to drive him around town delivering Christmas presents during the holidays. Although many years had passed since he was actively employed, the elderly man celebrated every Yule season by taking gifts to his former clients and colleagues. In the few days we spent together, I gained special appreciation for this retiree whose life was still fulfilling and productive because he was reaching out to others.

His generosity became more significant to me, and he became more real as a person when I realized that he was charitable in spite of the hidden burdens he was carrying. One afternoon as we were driving down the Pasadena Freeway he reflectively remarked that we were

But their physical limitations could not prevent their spirits from soaring.

passing the spot where his daughter had been killed in an auto accident a few years earlier. The grief of this tragedy was still fresh to the old man, yet he wouldn't allow his heavy sorrow to dampen his holiday spirit. I learned a valuable lesson from that encounter.

I picked up other jobs during high school that also gave me an appreciation for senior citizens. I spent one year driving an elderly woman on her Saturday errands. When I first met her I was appalled by her incessant smoking. But as we drove around town together, worked side by side in her rose garden, and shared afternoon snacks in her kitchen, I began to see her for who she really was. This woman had lived a life of tremendous joys, great accomplishments, and deep sorrows. As I spent time with her, my appreciation for all senior citizens grew tremendously.

I worked for another elderly man in our neighborhood who needed help around the house. He taught me how to use various tools in his workroom that his frail body no longer permitted him to use. One day he sold his house and moved to a retirement home where, shortly thereafter, he died. One of my greatest regrets in life is that I never visited him in that place.

My only comfort over this thoughtlessness is that I regularly participated in our church's outreach program to senior citizen centers. Our youth group often visited convalescent homes and hospitals where we conducted simple worship services. We sang songs, played our in-

struments, and shared testimonies with groups of patients who gathered in rooms filled to capacity. Most of these "parishioners" were confined to wheelchairs, and many could barely speak as a result of their weakened conditions. But their physical limitations could not prevent their spirits from soaring. It was not unusual to see tears in their eyes as they listened to our unsophisticated messages. While many could not participate in the singing, they often tapped their feet or nodded their heads in recognition of the old favorite hymns we sang. This was ministry in its purest form, and we received as much blessing from it as the seniors.

As a result of these interactions with the elderly, I never felt the generation gap or identified with those who talked about being alienated from their elders. Instead, I felt great love and respect for older people. I want my own children to have that same experience.

As parents we can help our children learn to know and love older people, to begin to appreciate their wisdom, and to feel the blessing of giving to others. We can provide them with opportunities to participate in nursing home ministry, to run errands for neighbors, to share with elderly family members and friends. And, best of all, these are things we can do *with* our children. The whole family can benefit.

A few years ago I came across a poem that was written by a woman who died in the geriatric ward of Ashludie Hospital near Dundee, Scotland. It was found among her possessions and was addressed to the nurses who cared for her in her final days. It says a great deal about the worth and needs of the elderly. May it encourage you and your children to spend more time with these very special people who are so often neglected.

"What do you see, nurse, what do you see?
Are you thinking when you look at me—
A crabbed old woman, not very wise,
Uncertain of habit with far away eyes,
Who dribbles her food and makes no reply
When you say in a loud voice—
      'I do wish you'd try.'

"Who seems not to notice the things that you do
And forever is losing a stocking or shoe,
Who resisting or not, lets you do as you will
With bathing and feeding, the long day to fill.
Is that what you're thinking, is that what you see?
Then open your eyes, nurse. You're not
      looking at me.

"I'll tell you who I am as I sit here so still.
As I move at your bidding, eat at your will,
I'm a small child of ten with a father and mother,
Brothers and sisters who love one another;
A young girl of sixteen with wings on her feet,
Dreaming that soon a love she'll meet;
A bride at twenty, my heart gives a leap,
Remembering the vows that I promised to keep;
At twenty-five now I have young of my own
Who need me to build a secure, happy home.

"A woman of thirty, my young now grow fast,
Bound together with ties that should last.
At forty, my young sons have grown up
    and gone,
But my man's beside me to see I don't mourn.
At fifty once more babies play round my knee
Again we know children, my loved one and me.
Dark days are upon me, my husband is dead.
I look at the future, I shudder with dread.
For my young are all rearing young of their own,
And I think of the years and the love
    that I've known.

"I'm an old woman now and nature is cruel.
'Tis her jest to make old age look like a fool.
The body it crumbles, grace and vigor depart.
There is a stone where I once had a heart.
But inside this old carcass a young girl
    still dwells,

And now again my battered heart swells.
I remember the joys, I remember the pain
And I'm loving and living life over again.
I think of the years, all too few, gone too fast,
And accept the stark fact that nothing can last.
So open your eyes, nurse, open and see
Not a crabbed old woman,
Look closer—see me!"

Indeed, many of those who participated in our survey do not see a crabbed old woman. They recognize the warmth, strength and depth of character that lies beneath the infirmed and frail shells of old age. Given my own early experiences with elderly people and those of my correspondents, it is evident that showing respect for the aged, treating them well, and appreciating their contributions has

Whatever we give the elderly,
we receive back tenfold.

its own rewards. Whatever we give the elderly, we receive back tenfold. We can learn from them, enrich our own lives by hearing about their experiences in this world, and deepen our own relationship with God through them.

We live in a society which values youth, almost above all else. To be forty is often considered to be over the hill. Countless people who would have years of service to give are forced to retire at age sixty-five. Untold numbers of older people are warehoused and ignored. While we may not be able to change an entire society's disrespect, we can teach our children to appreciate the elderly—for their benefit and for our kids' sake as well.

S

o in Christ we who are many form one body, and each member belongs to all the others.

Romans 12:5

The Blessings Of Church Life

It is entirely appropriate that involvement with a local church makes this list of values and principles we want to pass along to our children. Throughout Scripture God commands us to "Keep holy the Sabbath!" as a day of worship and rest. Furthermore, we are advised repeatedly about the benefits of life in a community of believers. Thus, many parents obviously feel regular church attendance should be an integral part of their children's upbringing.

One respondent to our survey reflected on her early experiences with church life: "My mother and father were strong Christians and were active in ministering in our church," she said. "They made sure that we attended church regularly and became involved in the youth activities and ministry. I cherish the years I spent in youth ministry. It was a good foundation for the activities I am involved with now as an adult."

I share this conviction because I realize that I am a product of my church heritage. I grew up in the same church for the first eighteen years of my life, and it literally defined me. I learned most of my spiritual lessons in that church. I also received cultural training there, including appreciation for music, drama, and public speaking. I learned about distant parts of the world from our missionaries who instilled in me the value of other races and less fortunate people. In church I developed lifelong friendships. In fact, I met my wife, Linda, in church. And, of course, in church I learned about Jesus and his love for me.

I grew up in a thriving medium-sized church, which was literally the center of our lives. My parents took us to services on Sunday mornings and evenings. On Wednesday nights they brought me to the mid-week children's club, and on Saturdays I participated in teen activities throughout my adolescence. When the church doors were open, our family was there with enthusiasm. The Memorial Day picnic, Vacation Bible School, summer camp, the annual Christmas program, and even routine fellowship hours were highlights on this little boy's calendar.

*Small churches offer intimacy,
care for others,
and life as a community.*

In effect, the church was a subculture that served as a safe harbor in an ungodly world. And today I want that more than ever for my own kids. I want them to experience the same nurturing and development that growing up in church provided me.

At the same time, I realize that life in the 1990s is far more complicated than it was thirty years ago. Kids today have more options and distractions that compete for their attention. The task of directing our offspring into church is more challenging than ever.

Our changing society presents other barriers toward this objective. A few years ago, I attended a church growth seminar and learned how our culture has redefined the concept of commitment. In previous generations, people dedicated themselves to a church and attended virtually every service faithfully. But today's families are under so much pressure, they often feel that commitment means once-a-month attendance.

I remember how, as a youth pastor, I struggled with parents who couldn't find time to bring their teenagers to church activities. Often, these same parents later wondered why their offspring turned their backs on the Christian faith.

When my wife and I started a family, we decided that we would never miss an opportunity to get our kids involved in the life, culture, and ministry of a church. We wanted our children to develop a passion for the Lord and his people.

A few years ago we moved into a new community and began looking for a place to worship. We tried every evangelical church in

---

In getting close to their church community they can learn invaluable lessons about God's love for them.

---

town, and we used a mental checklist to compare them all. We considered the size of these churches. While large congregations have obvious advantages, small churches offer intimacy, care for others, and life as a community that can't be duplicated by the mega-churches. These qualities can contribute more to the kids' well-being than all the sophisticated programs put together. In getting close to their church community they can learn invaluable lessons about God's love for them.

We also evaluated the pastor and his preaching, the choir and the music program, the Sunday morning worship service, the friend-liness of the people, the adequacy of the facilities, the number of people our own age, the particular theological distinctions, and the proximity to our home.

We looked for a place that taught sound doctrine and provided an opportunity for us to serve others. Most importantly, we wanted to follow the Lord's guidance. We knew he had a good church home for us.

But there was another criterion that weighed on our hearts. What was the overall quality of their children's ministry? Did they have a vibrant Sunday school? Was there an active children's choir? Did they celebrate the holidays with special presentations? Did they have dedicated leaders who cared for the kids? Was the nursery clean and well-managed? How was the Vacation Bible School and Bible Camp program? Perhaps it sounds rather calculating to approach the process this way. But I don't think it is inappropriate to ask these kinds of questions when evaluating which church is going to contribute to the spiritual training of your precious offspring.

The world is full of parents who are seeking churches that will nurture their children. That journey, if prayerfully considered, leads people to churches of various sizes and emphases. Hopefully, it will take them to congregations where there is a heart for reaching their kids. Every parent shares that concern.

We had a "Preparation Day."
We spent every Saturday getting ready
for the Sabbath.

In spite of our love for God's house, I must confess that Sunday mornings in our home are not the paradigms of harmony and reverence they should be. When I mentioned that I was writing on the subject of the Sabbath, my son, Peter, winced. "Oh brother," he said. Without uttering another word, he began shaking his head and walked out of the room. One would think from this reaction that I was about to describe something as horrific as a nuclear holocaust or the grisly process of making sausage.

Our Sabbaths are anything but restful. While most families on our block are rolling out of bed at a late hour and lingering at the breakfast table, we are making a mad dash to get ready for church. The house is buzzing with frantic activity as we all try to squeeze into the bathroom at once, gulp down our breakfasts, and put on our Sunday best. It would all be total chaos except for the sense of order that I contribute. I keep them all moving by regularly intoning the countdown to departure. "We're leaving in ten minutes! . . . We're leaving in five minutes! . . ."

By the time we hit the road, we're inevitably late, and confusion reigns in the car. We're all accusing one another of being most responsible for our tardiness. Someone has forgotten his Bible, someone else is still brushing her hair, and the baby has chosen this moment to dirty his diaper. In the background noise, my older son is rehearsing his assigned Scripture memory verse in nonstop monotone.

When things have finally settled down, my daughter speaks up: "Dad, we have just got to do a better job of getting ready for next Sunday," she lectures. Her brother chimes in, and they are soon talking about all the reasons why they can't afford to miss one minute of church. After all, today's class is very important, they explain, and they have rehearsals for the Christmas program, and they have so many friends they must see. It's clear that Sunday is a significant event in their lives. And this provides me with a great sense of fulfillment.

As we pull into the church driveway, the kids are opening the car doors before I've come to a complete stop. In an instant they are running toward their classrooms, full of excitement about the morning's activities awaiting them. A smile breaks across my face and I breathe a thankful prayer for this church and the hectic pace it puts us through every Sunday morning.

Perhaps our family should take the advice of one great-grandmother who replied to our survey on values: "In our home, we had a 'Preparation Day.' We spent every Saturday getting ready for the Sabbath. We laid out for each child the clothes they'd wear to services. Buttons were sewn on, socks were mended, clothes were laundered. 'Preparation Day' is a biblical concept and a precious one. It is good to prepare both physically and spiritually for the Lord's Day and will reduce Sunday morning hassles to a minimum. We filled the gas tank on Saturday. Set the Bibles out. It really didn't take all that long to prepare, and it was so rewarding."

Many people wrote to us about the rewards and benefits that regular church attendance gave them in their youth. One woman wrote poignantly, "Mom had two disastrous marriages by the time I was five and a half. When I was about twelve I asked Mother how she got involved in church. I'll never forget her answer. She said, 'I knew I wanted a better life for my little girl than the one I've had, so I knew I had to change my life, and that's when we began going to church.' Today, as a mother, I cannot begin to express my appreciation for my upbringing. I am so very thankful that God gave my mother the wisdom she needed at a very difficult time in her life."

Reading these letters is a tribute to the power of the church's influence on a young life. Perhaps this explains why God ordained it as one of two institutions vital to our survival (the other being the family).

Allow me to conclude this chapter with an essay entitled "Why Not Go to Church," by Dr. R. T. Kendall of Westminster Chapel in London. His comments strike at the heart of why church is a significant blessing for every believer:

Why not? You should not go to church because it is convenient. You should not go to church because the people are friendly. You should not go to church because the singing is good, the organist plays well, or because the preaching is interesting. You should not go to church because there are children the age of your own, or because you will make the deepest friendships you have ever known.

You should not go to church because our nation is in trouble or because the soul of our country is spiritually bankrupt. You should not go to church because your marriage is in difficulty or because your children are growing up without purpose. You should not go to church because no one really cares what happens to you.

Why should you go to church? Because you have a soul. Jesus said, "What good is it for a man to gain the whole world, yet forfeit his soul?" (Mark 8:36). What will you give in exchange for your soul?

You should come to church for the sake of your own soul. For if you lose your soul, you lose everything that ultimately matters.

I doubt you will ever read truer words!

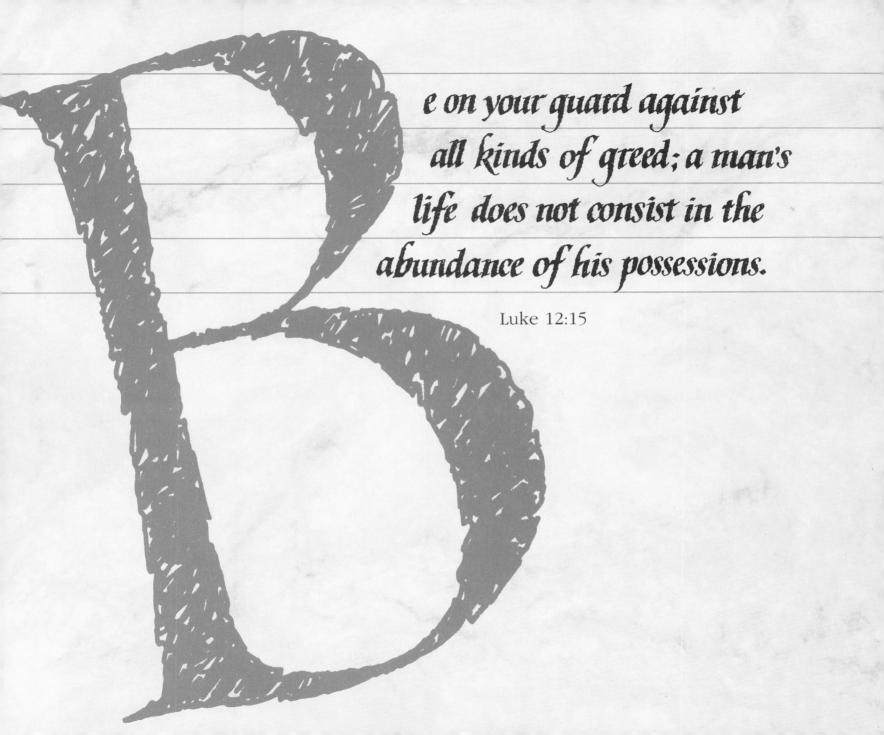

Be on your guard against all kinds of greed; a man's life does not consist in the abundance of his possessions.

Luke 12:15

Avoiding The Pitfalls Of Materialism

In the spring of 1990, I was traveling in England with my colleague Bruce Peppin when we had something I can only describe as a divine encounter. It occurred late one morning while we were on our way to a Christian booksellers' meeting in Blackpool.

We had stopped at a roadside cafeteria along the M-1 Highway for an early lunch. The restaurant was quiet at that hour, but we selected a table in a far corner where we could continue a conversation begun in the car.

In the middle of our meal, a man came and sat down next to us. I remember being irritated with him because he could have chosen thirty other tables in the nearly empty restau-

rant. Now we had no privacy. Unless we whispered, this man would hear everything we said.

Sure enough, three minutes later, he leaned over and said in a Scottish brogue, "Excuse me, but I couldn't help overhear your conversation. I can tell by your comments that you are Christians. My name is Phillip, and I also love the Lord."

He then explained that he had just returned from Rumania where he had led a caravan of trucks to deliver relief supplies to an orphanage. When Bruce and I introduced ourselves as members of the Focus on the Family ministry in America, his eyes nearly popped out of his head.

"This is truly remarkable," he exclaimed. "Yesterday in Rumania, I spoke to a man who gave me this piece of paper." Phillip handed us the note which was inscribed with a handwritten message: "Please send Dr. Dobson's materials to help us." The Rumanian's name and address were at the bottom.

"You are the first people I have met since returning to England," Phillip told us. "The Lord must have arranged for us to meet in this way. Let me share with you more about the work we are doing in Rumania." He then continued to describe the unbelievable conditions in the orphanages where little children are deposited by parents who are hopelessly enslaved by poverty. You could hardly imagine anything worse than being an inmate at one of these facilities. The children have no shoes, no clothes, no heat, no toys, no medical care, and almost no food. They live in absolute filth and are confined to rooms crammed with metal cribs. He showed us pictures of babies in tattered gray diapers standing on urine-soaked mattresses. "They desperately need the basic necessities of life," Phillip said. "But most of all, they need love and affection."

Our hearts burned with conviction and our eyes were swollen with tears. We believe that the Lord had indeed arranged this encounter, and we were determined to help, even though Focus on the Family is not a relief organization (there are many fine ministries better equipped

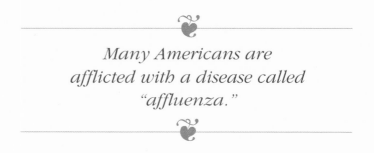

Many Americans are afflicted with a disease called "affluenza."

and dedicated to this purpose). When we returned from our journey we made arrangements to provide some assistance to this tremendous problem. Since then, we have visited this orphanage and noted a general improvement in their condition.

We can hardly look at such poverty and deprivation without comparing them to the abundance and materialism in Western society. While much of the Third World suffers from malnutrition and starvation, many Americans are afflicted with a disease called "affluenza." In this country, we are infected at birth. Typical middle-class newborns have a nursery full of Fisher-Price toys, stuffed Disney animals, baby furniture, colorful books, and musical cassettes.

As they grow older, our children become acquirers of other brand-name toys like G.I. Joe, Nintendo, Barbie, and Ninja Turtles. Well before adolescence, they want designer label clothes, compact discs, and videotapes.

By the time our kids reach adulthood, they will be trapped on a merry-go-round whose only reward is a golden ring of champagne wishes and caviar dreams. Their houses will be cluttered with gadgets, adornments, and other needless stuff accumulated along the way.

I know because our family has boxes of junk in the garage that we have moved from one home to the next without ever opening. Don't ask me why I keep dragging those useless possessions through life! I am by no means wealthy, but I have been affected by the materialism that plagues our nation.

In the popular movie *Wall Street*, the character played by Michael Douglas declares his personal philosophy: "Greed is good. Greed works." He could have been speaking for the entire society. I'm sick of seeing this bumper sticker everywhere I go: HE WHO DIES WITH THE MOST TOYS WINS.

Our materialism has produced a nation of gluttons who own everything but the concepts of deferred gratification and modesty. I recently received a letter from a young man in prison who was convicted for check fraud. He went into debt acquiring the things he couldn't afford. When his checks started bouncing, he tried to cover them by drafting checks from another account in an out-of-state bank. Eventually it all caught up with him, and he was thrown in jail.

This poor man's life was ruined by a desire for things which have no substance. He was seduced by the promise of pleasure only to find that it was a betrayal. I learned a valuable lesson about such vain pursuits when I was invited to dine with a friend at one of Washington, D.C.'s exclusive restaurants. My host was an executive who managed this establishment,

---

Materialism is like the golden dome that pleases the eyes, but its contents leave us hungry for something else.

---

and we received the red-carpet treatment the entire evening. I had never eaten in such an elegant environment.

We were ushered to our table by a French maitre d' who had an army of waiters and busboys at his command. Attentive uniformed servers were stationed behind us and refilled our glasses after every swallow. Our table was decorated with a beautiful white linen cloth, silver cutlery, and a fantastic floral centerpiece. Prior to our meal, my friend explained the research that had formed the restaurant's philosophy for service. "We have learned that the presentation is more important than the meal itself," he said. Thus, the decor, the service, and the way food is arranged on the plate have greater significance than the quality or taste of the meal. The theory was that people are more satisfied by their eyes than their palates.

Suddenly the main course arrived with considerable fanfare. There was one waiter for each person in our party. In unison the waiters laid a plate covered with a golden dome on the table in front of each guest. Then the maitre d' reappeared and stood at the head of our table. Like a symphony conductor, he gave a majestic flip of his wrists, and the waiters all moved at once to remove the domes and reveal the entrees. Voilà! Such drama. What a great presentation! The host was beaming.

But then something unexpected occurred.

After a few moments of silent confusion, everyone simultaneously looked up from their plates and said, "That's not what I ordered!" So much for the big moment.

Materialism is like the golden dome that pleases the eyes, but its contents leave us hungry for something else. Fortunately Americans seem to be discovering this lesson after years of binging on gaudy consumerism. A Time/CNN poll in 1991 revealed that people are forsaking the status symbols, the rampant buying, and the unbridled ambition of the gilded 1980s. This survey found that a vast majority of people would like to slow down and live a more relaxed life. When asked about their priorities, 89 percent said it was more important these days to spend time with their families than to earn a high salary.

Time magazine reported on one woman's transformation:

Marsha Bristow Bostick of Columbus remembers noticing with alarm last summer that her three-year-old daughter Betsy had memorized an awful lot of TV commercials. The toddler announced that she planned to take ballet lessons, followed by bride lessons. That helped inspire her mother, then thirty-seven, to quit her $150,000-a-year job as a marketing executive. She and her husband, Brent, a bank officer, decided that Betsy and their infant son Andrew needed more parental attention if they were going to develop the right sort of values. Marsha explained, "I found myself wondering, *How wealthy do we need to be?* I don't care if I have a great car, or if people are impressed with what I'm doing for a living. We have everything we need."

Many experts, including market researchers and sociologists believe this movement away from materialism is more than a temporary fad. "I'm impressed by how deeply it goes into the fabric of this country," said one. An advertising agency that studied the trend reported that "everything important seems to be tied directly to children." In other words, parents are moving away from godless consumerism because they recognize the impact it is having on their offspring. Either it robs them of time with their kids, or it instills corrupt values in them.

Does all this mean that we shouldn't care about our possessions? A few years ago, my wife and I were house hunting in Southern California. After days of searching we finally found a home that had everything we wanted for a price we could afford. It wasn't a large house, but it was in immaculate condition. Everything

from the window coverings to the garden demonstrated the owners' loving care.

One evening we returned to the house for a closer inspection and to ask the sellers some questions.

"You certainly have a beautiful home here," I said to the woman of the house.

"Well, thank you," she replied, "but it is not as nice as it looks."

I raised one eyebrow at the strange comment and decided she had just chosen her words poorly.

"You must spend a lot of time in the backyard," I said. "The gardens are gorgeous."

"Yes, but we have a terrible time with poor drainage in the winter. After a good rain this whole lot is flooded for days."

"Oh really," I muttered. After an awkward pause I continued the conversation. "We like the fact that this house is only two blocks from the local elementary school."

"Oh, you don't want to send your kids there," she exclaimed. "It used to be a nice school, but now the classrooms are overcrowded, and they have tremendous discipline problems."

"Is there anything else you would like to warn me about?" I asked.

"Well, only that there has been a rash of crime in our neighborhood lately," she said. "We've had several bicycles stolen on this street in the past few weeks."

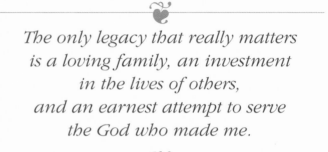

The only legacy that really matters is a loving family, an investment in the lives of others, and an earnest attempt to serve the God who made me.

It was the weirdest conversation I had ever had with someone who wanted to sell something to me. But the next day we learned that this woman loved her home and didn't want to part with it. This house was her homestead where she had raised her family and established many happy memories.

Certainly we could understand that emotion. Her attachment to that home was not materialism as much as maternalism. There is nothing wrong with having nice things or feeling pride of ownership. Scripture only warns us to recognize the temporary value of earthly possessions. Christ said, "For where your treasure is, there your heart will be also" (Luke 12:34).

All parents love the reward of watching their children open presents. There is nothing like the wide-eyed excitement of a little boy or girl who sees a much-desired toy when the wrapping paper has been torn away. It is a natural desire of parenthood to want to give our kids every good gift and every possible advantage. But we need to seek a balance, because we can destroy our children with materialism.

I recently read the story of a young man whose grandfather built a family fortune and lavished his descendants with wealth. "As a child my real contacts were with maids," the man said. His father was an alcoholic who self-destructed at an early age, and his mother, who had married into the family, was uncomfortable with the money and power that came with her marriage. Under these circumstances, the man said, "You end up bonding with a set of images: your parents, whom you don't know; the servants, whose real lives and feelings you know nothing about; and the legendary family name, which somehow feeds everybody."

Few of us have to worry about the problems associated with this kind of an estate. However, this man's tragic story conveys an important message for those who believe that money will bring happiness and meaning.

Early in my relationship with Dr. Dobson we were in Phoenix for a speaking engagement. One night our hosts took us on a tour of the elegant Wrigley Mansion, which sat on a high hill overlooking the city. "Isn't this an incredible place?" I asked as we gazed at the magnificent view before us.

Dobson's response surprised me. "I am not impressed," he said. "This empty house is just a monument to man's impermanence. The only legacy that really matters is a loving family, an investment in the lives of others, and an earnest attempt to serve the God who made me."

May that be the lesson we teach our children about the true substance of life.

You shall seek me and find me when you seek me with all your heart.

Jeremiah 29:13

Building Our Children's Faith Through Worship

As a child Dr. Dobson was greatly influenced by his great-grandmother, a godly woman who found ways to fill his life with spiritual applications. One afternoon, when he was five years old, Jim was in the backyard with her. A plane flew overhead, and the excited boy shouted, "Look, grandma, there's an airplane!"

"Oh, we should pray for the pilot in that plane," she said. "That person is known to God and has special feelings and needs. We should ask the Lord to give that pilot a safe journey."

At that moment under a sunny sky, little Jim joined hands with his great-grandmother and prayed for a person they had never known and would never see again. To her, this inci-dent may have been nothing more than an-other simple expression of faith. To the boy, it taught a lesson in prayer that he vividly re-members more than fifty years later.

This story also has a message for many parents who responded to our survey on spiri-tual values. I read scores of letters from moms and dads who want to teach their children the importance of having a life committed to prayer and worship. To accomplish this objective, we must allow our children to observe our faith in action. We will have an impact on them if we can demonstrate that prayer is a significant part of our lives.

I know this from personal experience. There is a picture in my mind that I can never erase. It was etched there when I was twelve years old. Our family had traveled to Sweden where we visited many relatives I had never

We can be assured that our children are observing our prayer life and its impact on our lives.

met before. One night we stayed with my maternal grandparents at their home in Stockholm. The next morning I rose early and thought I was the only one who was awake in the house. I wandered into a room where I found my grandfather on his knees seeking the Lord. I can still see him, bowing over a sofa with his face in his hands as he quietly prayed. Because of our geographical distance from each other I never really knew this man very well. But the image in my memory tells me that he was a man of prayer and has always challenged me to imitate his example.

Many people wrote to tell me that they have similar remembrances and were deeply affected by them. One woman wrote, "Mom never began a day's work without first sitting on the edge of her bed reading her Bible and praying. Many other things clamored for her attention, but she had an appointment to keep."

In his book, *How to Keep Your Kids on Your Team,* Charles Stanley, senior pastor of the First Baptist Church in Atlanta, described how his prayer life affected his children:

Many times my children would open my study door and see me stretched out on the floor praying. Most of the time they would close the door quietly and leave. Sometimes, though, Andy or Becky would come in, tiptoe over to where I was, and stretch out beside me. Andy wouldn't say anything, but Becky would wait for a while and then whisper, "Dad, I have a little problem. Could we pray about it together?" I have always believed that two of the most important things I could ever teach them were the importance of prayer and how to pray. I guess the old saying, I'd rather see a sermon than hear one any day, is still true. My children probably could not tell you much of what I have said in sermons on prayer (and I have preached a lot on the subject), but they have both told me that they will never forget seeing me stretched out before God, talking to him about whatever was on my heart. So I know that the best way you can teach your kids to pray is by your example.

In the confines of our homes, we can be assured that our children are observing our prayer life and its impact on our lives. One woman recounted how she unknowingly influenced her children through her habit of daily devotions. One year at Christmas she asked her children to buy her a new Bible because she had worn hers out. One of her daughters-in-law asked her, "Would you still leave the old one on the coffee table where we're accustomed to seeing it? As I saw your Bible wearing out over the years, I watched you become a happier person. Would you leave it there as a reminder to us of your relationship to God?"

Jamie Buckingham, a columnist in *Charisma* magazine, shared a similar story of how his parents' prayer life affected him. Not long ago, he met with his siblings to divide the property they inherited when their father died and their mother moved into a retirement home. He said:

I wanted only one thing: the tattered "prayer book" that my parents had used every morning for years. Actually, it was an oversized photo album with seven pages—one for each day of the week. Each page contained the pictures of those they prayed for that day. My dad had made a little stand so that the album could stay open on the breakfast table, and each morning before eating their meager breakfast, they prayed for their friends.

I took the old book and sat on the back steps, looking at each page.

Monday, they prayed for their local Gideon chapter—an organization dedicated to the distribution of Bibles.

Tuesday, they prayed for the Billy Graham organization—and for Billy's crusades.

Wednesday, they prayed for Tom and Betsy Smoak, then missionaries with Wycliffe Bible Translators in Colombia, South America. I recall sitting at breakfast with them, listening as my mother's voice broke with emotion as she prayed for the six Smoak children by name.

Thursday, they prayed for two elderly women who had given their lives as missionaries to mountain people in Appalachia.

Friday, they prayed for old friends.

Saturday, a family picture helped them remember all their children and grandchildren.

Sunday, even after they were too feeble to attend, they prayed for their local church, and for the staff and residents at the retirement center.

Now mother was in that same center. The

book had been left behind.

I took it home. It remains in my study, closed. The stand, however, is on our breakfast table. It holds *my* prayer book—complete with pictures.

While it is important to model the act of prayer and worship, we must also not forget the substance of these actions. Jesus reminded us that God is eager to answer our petitions. "If you, then, though you are evil, know how to give good gifts to your children, how much more will your Father in heaven give good gifts to those who ask him!" (Matthew 7:11).

Several of my correspondents described how God answered the prayers of faithful parents who sought the salvation of their offspring. "When I was truly and completely converted," one woman said, "I realized that my grandmothers had prayed steadfastly for a quarter of a century for me. One of them died before I was saved. Yet her prayers rose as a remembrance before God's throne. So a heritage of prayer is their gift to me, realized in my own salvation. Do you suppose I will ever give up praying for my children, or my husband, or some day, my grandchildren? Not likely!"

As one person said, "As long as there is life, there is hope. Because with God all things are possible. Prayer works!"

Our children will learn about the power of prayer if we include them in our devotional lives. Within reason, we should share our burdens with our children. We should allow them to join us as we pray about financial hardships, health problems or other needs. Let them get on their knees with us and watch the Lord answer our prayers. Nothing will cause our children's faith to grow stronger!

Finally, let me say a few words about another form of worship that is integral to every child's spiritual training. We have found that music is a particularly effective way to speak to the Lord.

I realized that my grandmothers had prayed steadfastly for a quarter of a century for me.

Our family once spent four beautiful days at Lake Powell in Utah. The trip proved to be a refreshing disengagement from our hectic lifestyle. But more importantly, it gave us much

quality time with our children, who are growing up so quickly.

During our trip, I also confirmed a suspicion I had about our kids' Christian worship experience. While driving across Arizona, I played a cassette recording of hymns on the car stereo. To my dismay, our children were completely unfamiliar with this collection. My wife and I had known these songs since earliest childhood, and yet *our* children were completely ignorant of them.

One night during our trip, my daughter, Viveca, and I were gazing at a star-filled sky. I was immediately reminded of "How Great Thou Art."

O Lord my God,
When I in awesome wonder
Consider all the worlds Thy hands have made,
I see the stars,
I hear the rolling thunder,
Thy pow'r thruout the universe displayed!

As I sang this familiar hymn, I realized it was brand new to Viveca. But she eagerly picked up the melody and words, and it became an anthem for the rest of our holiday.

When I returned home, I called Wes Haystead, a curriculum consultant to Focus on the Family, and asked if hymns are slipping in

---

*Let them get on their knees
with us and watch
the Lord answer
our prayers.*

---

popularity. "Yes," he responded. "Usage is declining dramatically. Of course, old songs are always being replaced by new ones as music tastes change, but the current trend is more pronounced." Why? Haystead attributes it in part to the decline in use of the King James Version and other more formal expressions of worship.

My good friend Chuck Fromm, president of Maranatha! Music, agrees: "In previous generations, hymns were one of the primary ways to teach doctrine. They have been a very functional part of the church for the past two hundred years, but now kids are learning contemporary music, which is more conducive to modern media." In other words, the hymnal has been replaced by videos and overhead transparencies.

Some might argue that I am overly sentimental by clinging to old hymns, but I think my impulse to teach hymns and my concern that they're not being taught is valid for several reasons. First, there is tremendous value in tradition. Passing sacred songs from one generation to the next teaches our children about spiritual heritage. Our faith is validated in part because it has endured through the ages. Old hymns reinforce that lesson.

Second, these songs are beautiful poetic expressions that make a cultural contribution to our offspring. They need more creative enrichment than they receive from typical children's songs.

Third, many of the hymns have a substance that isn't found in the repetitive choruses we sing today. The devotional significance of the old songs—"Blessed Assurance," "Leaning on the Everlasting Arms," and "It Is Well with My Soul"—has been meaningful to me in many different circumstances.

Finally, these old hymns teach us to pray and deepen our prayer life. They enhance our relationship with the Lord. Martin Luther allegedly said he didn't care who preached the sermon as long as he wrote the song. He recognized the staying power of music in the worship experience. I believe that's an important lesson for all Christian parents in the spiritual training of children.

A

nd he took the children in his arms, put his hands on them and blessed them.

Mark 10:16

A Christian Children's Bill Of Rights

Certainly the preceding chapters can not presume to capture all of the significant values that our children must learn to lead spiritually productive lives. But it has been my hope that this list, which represents collective wisdom, provides a place to start for those who are blessed with the task of parenting. With this acknowledgment of incompleteness, I still feel compelled to add a final chapter that describes other basic precepts we owe our children.

In the Old Testament we read how children cherished and even strived for their parents' blessing. While the formal act of bestowing a birthright upon a child is no longer practiced, there are many blessings parents to-day can pass to their children—in addition to the values I have described.

As the father of a fourteen-year-old son, an eleven-year-old daughter (who thinks she's a teenager), and an inquisitive one-year-old infant (who will hopefully benefit from my experience with his older siblings), I'm always grateful for advice from more experienced parents. Recently I profited from a conversation with my good friend Robert Wolgemuth, who has raised two daughters through adolescence.

We were talking about the challenges of the dating years when Robert described two ground rules he and his wife, Bobbie, had established in their home. First, they decided their two daughters could not date before the age of sixteen. Second, Robert wanted to meet the prospective young man prior to the date.

Not long after their youngest daughter's sixteenth birthday, the first suitor came along, and Robert requested the obligatory interview. An appointment was arranged, and one evening the nervous lad came to the Wolgemuth home. As they sat down in the study for a man-to-man chat, it was clear the boy was perplexed by the necessity of this meeting.

Then Robert posed this question: "If a stranger came to your door and asked to borrow your car for an evening, would you give him the keys?"

"Well, no, of course not," the young man replied.

"I guess I feel the same way about your taking my daughter out on a date," Robert said. "I don't know anything about you, and yet you are asking to escort one of the most precious people in my life. Before I let you take her out, I want to know more about you—what you believe, your intentions and your character."

As I listened to Robert's story, I was reminded of the protective nature that we all feel as parents. Our kids are growing up in a crazy society, and we feel compelled to guard them.

We are forced to take precautions that would have seemed unreasonable a generation ago.

But our world is a different place today, and there are many strangers at the door who want to take our children out for a ride into the night. One example of the dangers our children face surfaced in a 1991 report from the Centers for Disease Control. This survey said that teen girls are twice as likely to have premarital sex today as they were in the permissive 1970s. This disturbing news is compounded by the growing epidemics of sexually transmitted diseases that are plaguing our young. All of these developments have occurred in spite of our massive efforts in sex education.

It's not only sex we need to worry about, of course. Teenage alcohol and drug use is equally disturbing and life-threatening. Given this environment, parents need all the help they can get to defend their offspring from harm. Unfortunately, that task is getting more difficult every day. Parents must not only fight the evil influences of secular society, but they are actually opposed by people who want to wrest parental control away from them. There is a growing philosophy in our society that children need freedom from adult leadership. Consider the fact that in many parts of the country, parental notification is no longer required when a daughter undergoes an abortion. So as the world becomes a more dangerous place, parents have increasingly less freedom and encouragement to protect their kids.

In his book, *Straight Talk,* Dr. James Dobson describes the dangerous points that are part of a bill of rights proposed by so-called child advocates. They included:

1. Children should have the right to make *all* their own decisions.

2. Children of any age should have the right to vote.

3. Children should have access to any information that is available to adults.

4. Children should be permitted to engage in any sexual activity that is legal for their parents.

5. Children should never be spanked under any circumstances.

6. Children of any age should be permitted to join a labor union, seek employment, receive equal pay for equal work, sign legal contracts, manage all of their own money, and be financially independent.

Now you may think this is just a way-out set of theories that will never see the light of day. But the Children's Rights Movement, as it is called, has gained steady momentum in recent years. The first major triumph for the movement

---

There is a growing philosophy in our society that children need freedom from adult leadership.

---

occurred in Sweden in 1979 when it became illegal for parents to spank their children. An emergency twenty-four-hour phone line was established by the Swedish parliament so kids could report their parents' violations of this law. A few years later, the Swedish government amended its Constitution to grant children the right to "divorce" their parents.

This philosophy has crept into American culture as well. Focus on the Family has interviewed many parents who have lost custody of their children for nothing more serious than giving them a well-deserved spanking. The legitimate problem of child abuse has given Children's Rights activists the opportunity to erode parental authority under the banner of social welfare. Some have called this trend "parent abuse." This growing movement seeks to give children unlimited independence from their mothers and fathers. Under the proposed panacea, kids are entitled to make significant spiritual and moral choices without the involvement of their parents.

These developments beg the obvious question: What are a child's basic rights? When we consider this question from a biblical and traditional perspective, we emerge with far different conclusions than those currently being advanced by our lawmakers and social scientists.

I suggest here an alternative—A Christian Children's Bill of Rights:

1. Every child has the right to receive spiritual training. All youngsters are entitled to learn about God and their relationship to him. They should know God as their Creator, Jesus as their Savior, and the Holy Spirit as their Comforter. Memorizing John 3:16—"For God so loved the world that he gave his one and only Son, that whoever believes in him shall not perish but have eternal life"—and singing "Jesus Loves Me" should be part of

each child's catechism. Every boy and girl should be dedicated at the altar and raised under the influence of the church.

Virtually all children have a period of vulnerability when they will believe almost anything they have been taught.

In a "Focus on the Family" broadcast, Dr. Dobson talked about the opportunity parents have to teach spiritual truths to their children. He explained that virtually all children have a period of vulnerability when they will believe almost anything they have been taught. For example, children who are between two and five years old will readily accept the notion that Santa Claus can fly all over the world on a single night and deliver gifts through chimneys to every good person. Our offspring unquestionably adopt the spiritual values we impart to them during these important years.

At the age of five or six, children become much more critical in their thinking, and their feelings about their Christian faith either become rooted in reality or they don't. If parents miss this window of intellectual development, they will find it much more difficult to teach biblical truths to their offspring later on.

"If you allow the first six years to pass without any religious training your children will be less likely to embrace spiritual concepts and behaviors," Dr. Dobson said. "That's why the Bible says, 'Train up a child in the way he should go, and when he is old, he will not depart from it'" (Proverbs 22:6).

2. *Every child has the right to physical nurturing.* At the age of six, my daughter, Viveca, became ill with a serious kidney infection. She was admitted to the hospital where an IV was inserted in her small hand to provide her with badly needed medicine and nourishment. One night when she woke from her fever, I was sitting next to her bed. I drew close to her and said, "Honey, what can I give you right now that will help you? I'll give you anything you want."

I thought she might want some more ice chips to cool her dry mouth. Perhaps she was ready for a cold drink or a fresh wet towel to hold against her hot forehead.

After considering my offer, she opened her heavy eyes. Then, in a voice that was barely above a whisper, she said, "I want . . . I want . . . a thousand Barbies!"

There she was, in the midst of a terrible fever, and all she wanted was a lifetime supply of dolls. I suppose that's why kids need parents. If they were left to their own devices, our children would try to sustain themselves with toys, candy, and such—or at least to bargain for extras when they see an opening.

I believe every youngster deserves to have nutritious food, a clean environment, and adequate shelter. These are the basic physical necessities of life, and all children are entitled to them.

Train up a child in the way he should go, and when he is old, he will not depart from it.

In addition, our offspring, have the right to receive good health care. They should have regular visits to a doctor and a dentist where they can receive preventive treatment. No child should grow up without hearing the familiar admonitions: "Eat your vegetables, brush your teeth, and wash behind those ears!"

3. *Every child has the right to be protected from abuse.* It is a sad commentary that this even needs to be mentioned, but it is a growing problem in our society. Children are suffering from sexual, physical, and emotional abuse in increasing numbers. Sadly, people who have been battered in childhood often repeat this pattern of abuse with their own offspring. A tragic legacy of violence begins that is then passed on through generations. These victims also find it difficult to receive God's love because they never experienced wholesome affection from their parents. Sexual abuse is also on the rise.

Some experts estimate that 25 percent of all women have been victims of sexual molestation during their childhood. At Focus on the Family, we receive heartbreaking letters from women who describe the lifelong devastation created by these experiences. No tender child should be exposed to this kind of perverted behavior.

A few years ago, I read an article in the *New York Times* about the child prostitution that is so prevalent today in the Philippines. It started in the 1970s when a Hollywood film company visited that part of the world to shoot a major production. Several members of the crew were homosexuals, and they offered valuable American currency to local parents for the right to have sex with their sons. Many impoverished parents accepted the money, and a child prostitution industry was launched that continues to the present time. These parents and the customers who pay them are guilty of the worst kind of child abuse.

Such unbelievable atrocities are a fulfillment of the reprobate society described in Romans 1:21-32. May God deliver us.

4. *Every child has the right to be protected from adult vices.* I recently visited a local video store where I saw to my amazement several X-rated titles located directly behind the counter at eye-level. I complained to the clerk, who merely shrugged his shoulders and said it was beyond his control. I persisted and asked to see the manager. When he arrived, there happened to be a little girl standing next to me. I said, "I think it's highly inappropriate for you to display those kinds of videos where a small child like her can see them."

He feebly explained that they had only placed these videos in a position dictated by their new computer inventory system. He acted as though he was helpless to do anything about it. I calmly told him that unless he changed the display, I would not bring my business back to him. The next day I returned and observed that all the X-rated videos were gone!

The point of my lone protest was essentially to safeguard the eyes of children from material that is inappropriate for them. Anyone who has seen Dr. Dobson's video interview of Ted Bundy cannot forget the condemned man's testimony of how he was affected at a young age by pornography. Just hours before his execution, Bundy recalled how his violent attitudes toward women began in adolescence when he started reading detective magazines that he found in garbage cans. We can never underestimate the power of such forces on the impressionable minds of our young. For Ted Bundy, these forces fueled a twisted fantasy life that led him to murder at least twenty-eight women.

Although pornography is an obvious evil, there are other adult vices from which our children should be safeguarded. My wife and I have tried to teach our kids about the dangers of such practices. When Viveca was five years old she had a basic understanding that smoking and drinking were bad habits which should be avoided. One night while eating in a restaurant we noticed that she was staring at a man who was smoking a cigarette. She then turned toward us and with an alarming look on her face she whispered, "Alcoholic!" At her level of understanding, she had equated cigarette smoking with alcoholism.

Our kids have the right to be protected from vices like pornography, alcoholism, drugs, and gambling. As parents it is our responsibility to create an environment devoid of these addictions and to warn our kids about their consequences.

5. Every child has the right to be a child. One of the consequences of our microwave-paced society is the tendency to rush our children into adulthood. I read about the Dollars and Cents Summer Camp program in Florida where kids as young as eleven learn how to invest in mutual funds and stocks and bonds. Apparently, many parents feel that childhood is not to be frittered away with playtime or fun. Instead, we push our offspring into preschools, adult fashions, and sex education. By the time these pressure-cooked kids reach puberty they are expected to look and behave like adults.

❧

Growing up is difficult under the best circumstances.

❧

The breakdown of family structures has also contributed to this dilemma. In his book, *The Hurried Child*, Dr. David Elkind blames the high divorce rate for forcing millions of children into adult situations. For example, aviation officials estimate that half a million children, some as young as five, fly alone each year.

I recently heard about a flight attendant who was approached by one of these small passengers. She learned that he was flying across the country to meet his mother for the first time in a few years. He asked the flight attendant to stay with him until his mother picked him up because he couldn't remember what she looked like, and he didn't want to go off with the wrong woman!

Growing up is difficult under the best circumstances. And when we attempt to rush our offspring to adulthood, we can make childhood a miserable experience for them.

I always feel a tinge of guilt when I impatiently ask my children, "Why don't you grow up?" A little voice whispers to me, "Why don't you let them act their age? They'll have to face the pressures of adulthood soon enough."

6. *Every child has the right to receive an education.* Of course all children are entitled to be taught history, mathematics, English, science, and all the subjects that will prepare them for a meaningful adulthood. But it is also important that they learn some of these subjects from a Christian perspective. How can you divorce history and biology from the role that God has played in them?

Parents of children in public schools must be particularly vigilant. I recently attended a curriculum review meeting in our local district. The faculty had selected a new series of course materials and wanted parental input prior to implementation. I was horrified to learn the precepts upon which this curriculum was based. One of the foundational principles was: "The teacher is not responsible for giving the right answer."

When I challenged this supposition, I was told that there is a new philosophy in public education today.

"We believe that what is right for you may not necessarily be right for me," the faculty member said. "Furthermore, what is right today, may be wrong tomorrow. Finally, if I tell your child that he has the wrong answer, I may suppress his self-esteem."

I couldn't believe my ears. The school district was essentially abandoning the authority of its teachers because it had no confidence in its positions. As a result, a generation of students will feel real good about themselves, while learning nothing definitive. Obviously, this New Age philosophy will never prepare them for the real world.

How can you divorce history and biology from the role that God has played in them?

We may not always be able to prevent ill-conceived teaching in public schools, but we can mitigate its effect by being informed. We owe this to our children.

I also encourage parental participation in support groups like Moms in Touch, a prayer team ministry that is specifically designed for public schools. My wife, Linda, has been an active participant in this program and can attest to its being worthwhile.

Outside of the classroom, parents should be involved in their children's homework. My wife and I have also taken our children on special field trips to a printing plant, a cheese factory, a juice-drink manufacturer, and other places for the sake of learning. All of this is designed to communicate the high priority we place on education while giving us an opportunity to add a Christian emphasis on the subjects our kids are learning.

A little effort now will yield a lifetime of benefits. Our kids are entitled to this.

7. *Every child has the right to develop his or her talents.* If it is true that God has endowed each of us with unique skills and abilities, then our children deserve to discover them. We can begin this process by exposing them at a young age to museums, concerts, live theater, and sporting events. When they express an interest in a certain area, we should encourage them to pursue it. If we can afford it, we should provide music, dance, art, and sports lessons to our budding offspring. Often we can find church or community-sponsored programs available for very little money. Behind every accomplished musician or sports legend are parents who have sacrificed time and money to help their child succeed.

A Gallup Poll found that 76 percent of America's teenagers believe it is too easy for people to get a divorce.

Even if your children have no desire to become stars, they should receive certain basic lessons in order to function well later in life. For example, they should have swimming lessons, as well as basic art and music appreciation classes. If these are not provided by your school, then they are usually provided at low cost by subsidized community programs. We also owe our children the opportunity to develop their spiritual gifts by praying with them, making opportunities for them to serve and befriend the sick and the needy, and letting them experience the fellowship of our Christian family at church.

8. *Every child has the right to a stable home environment.* A stable home environment means one in which the parents are available to meet the emotional needs of their children. Children should also see that, although their parents may disagree and argue, they also reconcile and express their love for each other. Children should have the reassurance of meals served on time. They should be able to count on adults doing what they say they'll do—picking them up from school or not repeatedly postponing that special outing because work deadlines interfere. They also need consistency from mom and dad.

As previously mentioned, one of the greatest tragedies of modern times is the dissolution of the family. For the past two decades, we have become accustomed to a 50 percent divorce rate. Only now are we beginning to realize the consequences of such widespread marital failure on our young.

The evidence is plain from a number of different sources: A 1990 survey of seventeen thousand children by the National Center for Health Statistics revealed that children of divorce perform poorer in school and have more behavioral and psychological problems than children raised by both biological parents. A

1991 Gallup Poll reported that family problems are by far the most prevalent instigators of teen suicides.

Several studies have revealed that children whose parents divorce are more likely to experience trauma later in life. Among the problems are insecurity, the fear of abandonment, and a quest for control. A 1989 Gallup Youth Survey found that 76 percent of America's teenagers believe it is too easy for people to get a divorce. Similarly, 75 percent of these youth feel that most people who get divorced did not try hard enough to save their marriages.

This evidence stands in sad contrast to a George Barna Research poll which reported that two-thirds of adults today say it is better for parents to get divorced if their marriage is not working than to keep the marriage intact for the sake of the kids. In other words, the presence of children is not seen as a valid reason for keeping the marriage together.

Clearly children are victimized by divorce and more consideration must be given to their needs. Couples should work harder than ever to keep their marriages intact. If you are among the growing number of single parents in our society, then you must face these statistics with determination to provide as much stability for your children as possible. Regardless of the circumstances surrounding failed marriages, single parents must move beyond the guilt and realize that God can redeem any of our actions for his glory and can mend the fabric of a home that has been torn apart by divorce.

Implicit in all of the aforementioned birthrights is positive parental action. In fact, children can have no meaningful entitlements without the involvement of a loving mother and father. God has given parents the responsibility to protect and enhance the lives of their offspring. We can do that by teaching them biblical values and by granting them these blessings. No one else can do that job more effectively. Just ask any child.